Aquinas for Armchair Theologians

Aquinas for Armchair Theologians

TIMOTHY M. RENICK

ILLUSTRATIONS BY RON HILL

Westminster John Knox Press
LOUISVILLE • LONDON

Scripture quotations from the New Revised Standard Version of the
Bible are copyright © 1989 by the Division of Christian Education
of the National Council of the Churches of Christ in the U.S.A.
and are used by permission.

Book design by Sharon Adams
Cover design by Jennifer K. Cox
Cover illustration by Ron Hill

First edition
Published by Westminster John Knox Press
Louisville, Kentucky

This book is printed on acid-free paper that meets the American
National Standards Institute Z39.48 standard. ♾

PRINTED IN THE UNITED STATES OF AMERICA

02 03 04 05 06 07 08 09 10 11 — 10 9 8 7 6 5 4 3 2 1

Library of Congress Cataloging-in-Publication Data

Renick, Timothy Mark.
    Aquinas for armchair theologians / Timothy M. Renick ;
illustrations by Ron Hill. — 1st ed.
        p. cm.
    Includes bibliographical references and index.
    ISBN 0-664-22304-4 (alk. paper)
    1. Thomas, Aquinas, Saint, 1225?–1274. I. Title.

B765.T54 R46 2002
230'.2'092—dc21

                                                2001045367

Contents

Acknowledgments

I would like to thank my teachers at Dartmouth College and Princeton University—especially Ron Green, Jeffrey Stout, and the late Victor Preller—who so skillfully introduced me to Thomas Aquinas and who so diligently encouraged me to sample the many treasures to be found in his thought. I also would like to thank my students at Georgia State University who, in the years since, have challenged me to examine Aquinas anew and who have prompted me to find creative ways to make his sometimes dry writings entertaining. I hope that this volume represents, in some small way, the best of both valued influences.

Special thanks are owed to Joseph Incandela, who offered helpful comments on an earlier draft of this volume.

Timothy Renick
Atlanta, Georgia
August 2001

CHAPTER ONE

Beginnings: Thomas Aquinas's Life and Times

The human mind can understand truth only by thinking.

—Thomas Aquinas

Thomas Aquinas ranks among the three or four most influential thinkers in the history of not merely Christianity but of Western thought in general. Aquinas's theory of natural law shaped our modern concept of human rights. His views of the state supplied the model for the arguments of Thomas

Jefferson in the Declaration of Independence. His com-
mentaries on sex are still hugely influential (and pretty darn
interesting). His views on the justice of warfare and the status of noncombatants have been codified into international
law and can be found in U.S. military handbooks. Seven
hundred years after his death, his proofs of God's existence
are still among the most discussed by philosophers. And
the compromise he worked out between faith and reason—
his answer to the question, "How can I be a religious person and still accept the claims of science?"—is the answer
adopted by most modern Christians to this day.

If you're an average American, Christian or not, you
walk around spouting some of Aquinas's views, challenging
others, and never stopping to ask, "From where did they
come?" For better or worse, we are all Thomists—followers of Thomas Aquinas—to some degree.

How did a quiet, unassuming intellectual become so
important to the modern world? Like all thinkers whose
influence is great, Aquinas's prominence is in part a product of talent, in part a product of being in the right place
at the right time.

When Aquinas was born, Europe was emerging from the
so-called Dark Ages, a period when the life of the mind
often was suppressed and church authority dominated. In
A.D. 1100, a century before Aquinas's birth, a Frenchman
by the name of Peter Abelard tried to use reason to shed
light on Christian doctrine. Doing so in a brash and con-
frontational manner, Abelard soon found himself branded
a heretic and standing at a public burning of his books.
(Those were the days when people knew the etiquette of a
good book burning; they had the manners to invite the
author.) He also found himself standing, barely one might
guess, without testicles—an indication that these were
indeed harsh times for anyone who crossed those in power.

EUROPE AT THOMAS'S BIRTH...

His main opponent that evening (though not the instigator of his emasculation) was Bernard, a church leader who proudly proclaimed, "I believe though I do not comprehend," and who taught his fellow Christians to accept by faith all of the dictates of the church.[1] One should support accepted ideas blindly, Abelard's age seemed to say. Don't ask questions. Don't expect answers.

In the century that passed between the time of Abelard and that of Aquinas, however, the church came face to face with some unprecedented challenges. Universities with

3

powerful, new ideas were established at Oxford (founded
c. 1200), Paris (c. 1200), Bologna (c. 1200), Cambridge
(1209), and Naples (1224). The Crusaders were bringing
back not only booty from the Holy Lands but strange new
religious and intellectual ideas—the teachings of Islam.
What worked when Christianity was insulated and iso-
lated—telling people to accept the claims of the church
blindly and without question—became more difficult to
sustain. Islam didn't even accept the infallibility of the
Bible. How could Christianity prove its truth to a Muslim
or to a scholar at Oxford?

Aquinas had the answer: reason. If the truths of the
Bible and the truths of Christianity could be shown to have
a rational basis—for instance, if the existence of the Christian God could be shown to be not merely an article of
faith and a claim asserted by the Bible but also a dictate of
reason—then Christians could win the day against their
new challengers. They could show their claims to be more
than mere "beliefs." Christianity would become "truth,"

mandated by reason. It was a brash strategy. After all, reason would only vindicate Christianity if Christianity were true. But few people in Christendom at the time doubted that Christianity held the truth, least of all a young Italian by the name of Thomas Aquinas. What was needed was some way—and someone—to convince outsiders of this "fact."

This is where Aquinas comes into the picture.

Thomas Aquinas was born in Aquino—a small town between Rome and Naples—around the year 1225. (Fun fact to impress friends and family: Aquinas is technically not his last name but a reference to his town of birth. He might be more accurately called "Thomas of Aquino." All right, maybe this fact will not *really* impress friends and family.) One of seven sons of a middle-level public official, Thomas was sent to a Benedictine monastery at the age of five to serve as an oblate—sort of an apprentice monk. At the time, many families of means expected the eldest son to inherit the family home and station, subsequent sons to join the military, and last-born sons to become priests and monks. (As you can well imagine, this could sometimes prove to be a problematic system. Wasn't Attila the Hun a last-born son? Huns make lousy monks.) For Aquinas, the fit was perfect. He took to the life of the mind—soon allegedly explaining fine points of theology to his teachers—and by the age of fourteen was studying the liberal arts at the University of Naples. Here the young Aquinas was first exposed to the writings of the great Greek philosopher Aristotle (born c. 384 B.C.). Aristotle was the philosopher who perhaps most shaped Aquinas's thought. What is less well appreciated is how influential Aquinas was to Aristotle—or at least to the survival of Aristotle's ideas.

For centuries, Aristotle's works had been branded dangerous and summarily suppressed, even destroyed, by the

5

church. By 1000, some of Aristotle's great books had been completely lost to Europeans. (Check out the Umberto Eco novel—or the Sean Connery film version of the book—entitled *The Name of the Rose* for a fictionalized account of the medieval church's opposition to Aristotle's works.) When the Crusaders returned from sacking Muslim libraries in the Holy Land, they brought back copies of Aristotle's works translated into Arabic which had, for centuries, been read, discussed, and preserved by Muslim scholars. Aristotle's *Politics, Ethics,* and *Metaphysics* survived in all or in part because the Muslim world had protected them through Europe's Dark Ages.

And because of Aquinas. For although Aristotle's works were rediscovered by Christians via the Crusades, they still officially were judged to be dangerous materials by the

church. The god (or gods) of Aristotle did not seem to be the God talked about in the Bible. At times, Aristotle even implied that the world was eternal—thus contradicting biblical accounts of creation described in the book of Genesis. One of Aquinas's great contributions ultimately was to show how Aristotle's "pagan" arguments could serve to support crucial Christian beliefs, such as the belief in God's existence. But I'm getting ahead of my story.

After attending the University of Naples, Aquinas joined the monastic order known as the Dominicans. This choice was not greeted warmly by his family. The Dominicans were a newfangled Christian group founded by a Spaniard by the name of Dominic just a few years before. While the Benedictines (the religious order that Thomas's parents had selected for him) had tradition, property, and prestige, the Dominicans were most noted for their absolute vow of poverty. Individual friars owned no possessions and went out each day to preach and to ask people for the food that would sustain them. The Dominicans also stressed literacy and learning. While Aquinas was attracted to this simple life in which the mind was prized as a path to God, his good, middle-class family was horrified that a family member was out begging for food in the streets. It just wasn't proper. Aquinas had joined, his family thought, the thirteenth-century equivalent of a cult. They needed to "deprogram" him.

Two of Aquinas's brothers "kidnapped" him one night in an attempt to turn him against the Dominicans. Legend has it that the brothers hired a prostitute and locked Aquinas and her together in a room for the evening. If Aquinas could be tempted into breaking his vow of celibacy, his brothers reasoned, Thomas would have to, or perhaps even want to, leave the order. Aquinas's medieval biographer, Bernard Gui, writes, "So a lovely but shameless

girl, a very viper in human form, was admitted to the room where Thomas was locked, to corrupt his innocence with wanton words and touches."[2] It's safe to assume that Gui was no feminist. It's also safe to assume that Aquinas resisted the temptation (after all, he is *Saint* Thomas Aquinas). As the story goes, Aquinas pulled out a hot poker (no, "hot poker" is *not* a euphemism here; get your mind out of the gutter!) from beside the fireplace, and he fended off the prostitute's advances throughout the evening. He then drew a cross on the wall with his smoldering poker (this is beginning to sound like a Jackie Collins novel) and collapsed on the floor, weeping and begging God to "grant me the gift of constant virginity." Aquinas's wish apparently was granted. By most historical accounts, Aquinas never engaged in sex on that—or any other—night. As Gui more colorfully puts it, "From that time onwards, it was his custom to avoid the sight and company of women—except in case of necessity or utility—as a man avoids snakes."[3]

There is some irony in the fact that Aquinas, who perhaps more than any other thinker shaped Western views on sexuality (we'll see exactly how in chapter 6), remained celibate throughout his life. When Aquinas was sainted in 1323, Pope John XXII had some difficulty locating the miracles necessary for canonization. Somewhat desperate to find miraculous events in the rather sedate (okay, *boring*) life of a scholar like Aquinas, the pope turned to, yes, the hot poker incident as one of Aquinas's miracles.[4]

The rest of Aquinas's life was rather uneventful. He read. He wrote. He ate. In fact, he did a lot of all three. His Dominican brothers allegedly referred to Aquinas as "the dumb ox." The "dumb" part was a reference to his quiet demeanor. The "ox" part was a jab at his weight. Aquinas had a large appetite by some historical accounts (though others refute the claim). One story has it that his Dominican brothers fashioned a special desk for him made with a semicircular indentation cut out of the desktop so that he could position his large girth more easily to the writing surface.

But Aquinas's *intellectual* appetite was greater still. By almost all historical accounts, he was brilliant. According to Saint Antoninus, Aquinas "remembered everything he had read, so that his mind was like a huge library." When asked what was the greatest grace he had ever received, Aquinas allegedly replied, "I think that of having understood whatever I have read."[5] His incredible work, the *Summa Theologica* (roughly translated, the *Summation of Theology*) is over two million words long and one of the greatest (and *longest*) works of philosophical system-building ever created. Putting his encyclopedic mind to good use, Aquinas integrated the ideas of the Bible; Aristotle (whom Aquinas calls simply "the Philosopher" throughout); Augustine, Jerome, and other earlier Christian authors; the great Jewish philosopher Maimonides; Muslim thinkers such as Averroës and Avicenna; and countless others. If Christianity was to be, as it claimed, the universal church with the universal truth, it must not limit its debate to Christians. It should listen to the great minds of Judaism, Islam, and even the pagans. It should learn from the wise wherever they can be found. The novelty of Aquinas in the history of early Christianity is that he did just that.

When not writing (or eating), Aquinas gave sermons, and he taught as a professor at the newly founded and flourishing University of Paris. His lectures began at 6:00 A.M. and attendance was reportedly high—another indication that these times were indeed very different from our own.

The year before his death at the age of only forty-nine (all those 6:00 A.M. classes apparently took their toll), Aquinas had a rather mysterious experience. Some historians claim it was a mystical experience—an encounter with God. Others say that it was a stroke. One account claims that after this event, Aquinas declared, "All my work is like

straw." Whatever the details, Aquinas gave up his greatest earthly love, his writing, at that point and never completed the mammoth *Summa Theologica*. He died the next year in 1274.

Given Aquinas's status as the most orthodox of Christian figures today, you may find it surprising to learn that three years after Aquinas's death, the archbishop of Paris, Stephen Tempier, banned the reading and dissemination of the work of all of the "radical Aristotelians," in effect condemning Aquinas's teachings as heretical. While there was no book burning this time, Aquinas's favorable treatment of the pagan Aristotle and his reliance on reason were judged to be a threat to Christians. Tempier's denunciation was repeated by the archbishop of Canterbury. Thomism was, for all practical purposes, condemned.

Of course, this was to change. Aquinas's magnificent, rational defenses and clarifications of Christian ideas were simply becoming too useful to a church facing new challenges from without. As Aquinas warned: "Muslims and pagans do not agree with us in accepting the authority of any Scripture we might use in refuting them, in the way in which we can dispute against Jews by appeal to the Old Testament and against heretics by appeal to the New. These people accept neither. Hence we must have recourse to natural reason, to which all men are forced to assent."[6] With the emergence of Islam and the growth of a host of other new challenges, Christianity *needed* Aquinas. Aquinas's intellect was of such a high order, and his work was so challenging and complex, that it took a little time for Christian leaders to realize that Aquinas's ideas represented a defense of the church rather than a threat to it. When the change came, it was a dramatic one.

In 1323, only a few years after the Paris ban was lifted and a half century after Aquinas's death, the church initiated efforts to make Aquinas a saint. It wasn't easy. Even granting a miraculous quality to Aquinas's chaste night with the prostitute, there was still the problem of finding other miracles in Aquinas's humdrum life. To find one miracle, the church turned to one of Aquinas's great earthly loves, eating.

Soon before his death, ill and bedridden, Aquinas allegedly was asked by the nurse who was tending to him what he wished to have for dinner. "Herring," he replied. The nurse was heartbroken; she would be unable to fulfill the request of a dying man. It was summer, and the herring were not running. The nurse ventured to the market nonetheless just as a fishing boat was arriving, and what should be on board but herring! A second—admittedly rather pathetic—miracle had been found. Aquinas would become *Saint* Thomas—and eventually the namesake for half of the parochial schools in the United States. (Just remember: If you hope to be a saint someday, be sure to

order wisely next time you visit your local Red Lobster restaurant. Why not try the herring?)

Some Christians have argued that a far more appropriate miracle to cite would had been the miracle that is Aquinas's thought and writings. There have been few more brilliant minds in all of Western history. In the late 1800s, Pope Leo XIII declared Thomism to be the official theology of the Roman Catholic Church. On all issues about which the pope and councils had not specifically declared a stance, the Catholic believer was told to consult the teachings of Aquinas. His writings, the faithful were instructed, are the very definition of Catholic orthodoxy, if not in "every detail" then in their "substance." Leo urged bishops to "restore the golden wisdom of Thomas and to spread it far and wide for the defense and beauty of the Catholic faith, for the good of society, and for the advantage of all of the sciences."[7] The 1879 instruction of Pope Leo to Catholics still holds to this day. In fact, it was recently and forcefully reiterated by Pope John Paul II in his *encyclical, Faith and Reason.*

Whether or not you are Catholic, whether or not you are Christian, Aquinas has shaped the life you live, the ideas you hold, and the actions you perform. He changed the way we think about thinking—doing more to make intellectual pursuits respectable, even godly, than perhaps any other figure.

And to think, it all started with a hot poker.

Let's begin our exploration of Aquinas's thought with a look at the celebrated compromise he proposed—a cease-fire of sorts—between faith and reason.

CHAPTER TWO

Humans, Angels, and God

Aquinas's greatest contribution to Western thought is perhaps his simplest (as the most revolutionary ideas usually are): Faith and reason need not be enemies. Far from suppressing reason as a means to the truth, far from claiming reason is an obstacle to faithful existence, Christians should embrace it. In fact, Aquinas taught, the two have a symbiotic relationship.

Reason needs faith. Why? First, using reason to, say, prove that God exists takes time and smarts. Many people lack one or both. (Aquinas was polite—and politic—enough not to name names.) Many people find it much easier to consult the Bible or their local priest on a matter than to try to prove the point rationally. Second, there are a few truths about the cosmos that can never be discovered by reason. For instance, the idea of the Trinity, Aquinas thought, was beyond the grasp of reason. (He won't get an argument from many modern Christians on that one.) It is "revealed" by God and must be accepted purely as an article of faith. In a none-too-subtle attempt to get Aristotle off the hook for making the very un-Christian claim that the physical world is eternal, Aquinas cites the belief that the earth was created as a second instance of a truth known by revelation alone. Since reason cannot prove definitively how and when the earth came about, Aristotle was merely stating his opinion on the issue. Hence, Aquinas points out, Aristotle's philosophical system does not rationally require that one contradict the Genesis account of creation and accept that the earth had no origin. So faith is crucial, Aquinas tells us, to any properly functioning individual:[1]

> As a matter of fact, if man could know perfectly all things visible and invisible, it would be stupid to believe what we do not see. However, our knowledge is so imperfect that no philosopher has ever been able to make a perfect investigation of the nature of one fly. We read that a certain philosopher spent thirty years in solitude, so that he might study the nature of a bee. If our intellect is so feeble, then, isn't it stupid to refuse to believe anything about God other than what man can know by himself?[2]

So far, even the traditionalist Bernard would have little problem with Aquinas's argument.

But Aquinas went on to argue, with Abelard and against Bernard, that the reverse is also true: *Faith needs reason*. To understand how, we must grasp how Aquinas depicts the human being.

For Aquinas, human beings are unique, somewhat like the animals and somewhat like the angels but identical to neither.

Animals learn new information in a purely sensory manner. For instance, if your dog learns that her food is kept in a certain kitchen cabinet, it is because she *smells* the food there, *sees* you open the cabinet door to get it, and so forth. Her senses are simply and solely the means by which she acquires the new information.

Angels, Aquinas reasons, cannot possibly learn things in this manner. Why not? Angels have no bodies, no flesh. They are "noncorporeal" to use Aquinas's terminology. They thus have no eyes with which to see, no noses with which to smell. And yet clearly angels are smarter than

dogs. (Well, maybe not smarter than that Eddie dog on *Frasier*.) How then do angels learn? Not by the senses but by the "intellect," Aquinas argues.

Intellect is the ability to know truths intuitively, to experience things not in a sensory way but on a direct intellectual level. This is a strange concept to our modern minds, trained as we are by science to rely on our senses almost exclusively. For an angel to know by means of the intellect is somewhat parallel to the way that a human being might know that she is, for example, madly in love. The love that she is experiencing is not something she can see, smell, or even feel—at least not in the empirical sense of "feel," as to "touch." (Note that I am speaking here of her love itself, not the *object* of her love.) She knows that she is in love in a far more direct, immediate, and all-encompassing manner. For Aquinas, this is how angels, via the intellect, know and experience *everything* that they grasp. For instance, angels don't "see" God (since they lack physical eyes and God himself is not a physical entity), but they nonetheless know that God exists by experiencing him directly. Angels, Aquinas argues, are thus superb at knowing *metaphysical* truths—literally, truths that are *after* or *beyond* the physical realm. (I'll talk more about metaphysics in chapter 4.) Their intellectual makeup is perfectly suited to knowing nonphysical entities. Angels can know God or love far better than can your dog. They have much greater difficulty, however, knowing simple physical facts like "That table is red" and "His voice is loud." One interpreter of Aquinas suggests that, in Thomas's schema, angels make great metaphysicians but lousy physicians.[3] They lack the means to acquire simple, empirical information, and hence cannot be relied upon to diagnose physical ailments.

What does all of this have to do with human beings? Quite a bit, according to Aquinas. You see, humans are

unique in all of creation for having the ability to learn *both* by sensory means and by the intellect. We are, in effect, a middle ground between the animals and the angels. Like animals, we have physical bodies and hence eyes, ears, noses, and so forth. We thus can smell food, see color, and hear voices in a way that dogs can and angels cannot. (An important aside: When humans use their sensory abilities to draw general conclusions—for instance, "incandescent light bulbs always generate heat"—they are using "reason" according to Aquinas. Today we might call this "induction" or "empiricism.") On the other hand, like angels, we also can know things via an intellect, intuitively and directly. The mystic who experiences God directly—who becomes "one with God"—might be an example of this human intellect in action. The person who "knows" that she should do good and avoid evil—not because some physical punishment awaits her evil act but just because good is the right thing to do—would be a second example of such "intellectual" knowing in humans for Aquinas. A moral claim such as "it is wrong to do evil," Aquinas reasons, cannot be empirically established. (Many modern philosophers agree with this point when they argue that logically you cannot derive an "ought" from an "is." Just because drilling a tooth, for example, "is" a source of pain does not mean that we "ought" not to drill teeth.) The claim that "it is wrong to do evil" is not provable by empirical evidence; it is a truth known or intuited by the intellect.

Unfortunately, according to Aquinas, our intellect is far less developed than that of angels. Unlike the angels, we are not pure intellect. We have bodies, and with these bodies comes an abundance of sensory information that both adds to our grasp of the physical world around us and, unfortunately, at times confuses our intellectual understanding of the metaphysical world. (Such confusion will be a pivotal component in Aquinas's explanation for human sin, to be discussed a little later on.) The important point for Aquinas is that, as humans, we are creatures of *both* "intellect" (like angels) *and* "senses" (like animals). These are the tools that God has given us. How foolish we would be, argues Aquinas, not to use them.

This brings us back to the topic of faith and reason. It is by our intellectual *and* sensory/rational faculties that human beings are meant by God to understand the cosmos, according to Aquinas. This is just as true when the topic of study is God as it is when the topic is physical ailments or incandescent lightbulbs. Sure, we need to have faith. But we also need to go out into the world, look for physical, sensory evidence of God, and reason from this evidence toward religious conclusions. To fail to do so is to fail to utilize our created nature, and it leaves us to see only part of what God has set out in front of us. For example, while accepting God's existence as an article of faith (i.e., because the Bible or the church says so) is to be valued, a deeper (or at least different) understanding comes when we establish God's existence by rational means—precisely because we are, by design, rational creatures. For Aquinas, for a human to try to know God without using her rational faculties would be like someone trying to appreciate the *Mona Lisa* by merely feeling the painting with her fingers. Doubtlessly, she could learn *some* important things about DaVinci's work by touching the painting, feeling the brush strokes, and so forth. (Advice from personal experience: Don't try this at the Louvre; the guards tend to get very testy.) But she gains so much richer an appreciation of the painting when she simply opens her eyes and uses all of the resources available to her. This, in effect, was what Aquinas asked of his age: Open your eyes! Use the tools that God has given to you. Reason and intellect were the tools.

When making such arguments, Aquinas sounds (and is) very modern. He emerges as an intellectual ancestor to the moderate, contemporary Christian. Think, for example, of the mainstream Christian arguing against the supporter of faith-healing who refuses to employ modern medicine to cure a sick child. To refuse to use the tools that God has supplied to humans, both Aquinas and the modern Christian argue, is a sign not of faith but of foolhardiness. Science and medicine are a testimony, not a threat, to God's design. As Aquinas writes, "It is impossible for items that belong to reason to be contrary to those that pertain to faith." If the belief is "true," then faith has nothing to fear of it. If the belief is false, then it cannot be a dictate of reason.[4]

These are simple yet powerful concepts. Let's see how they changed the face of Christian thought.

One of Aquinas's most famous uses of reason and intellect in the religious arena (and one I already have alluded to) are his proofs of God's existence, the substance of which is taken from Aristotle. These proofs are often called the "Five Ways," because Aquinas offers five parallel versions of the same argument. Let's take a look at the first of the Five Ways, what Aquinas refers to as the "argument from motion."[5]

As with all of his proofs, Aquinas starts his argument with a simple, all but irrefutable empirical observation: Things move. There are things in the world around us that are in motion. He next uses his human reason to draw a more general empirical observation: "Whatever is moved must be moved by another." Whenever we see motion, he says, we can trace it to some prior cause. Things do not just move on their own; they must be moved. Think of a ball on a pool table. If the ball is in motion, you know that the motion must have been caused by some prior force: a cue stick or another ball

hitting it, your lifting the table to tilt the surface, a gust of wind, the vibrations caused by the stampede of people leaving the pool hall when a Backstreet Boys song comes on the jukebox, and so on. Again, Aquinas is on sound scientific footing, making use here of a principle that would later become a cornerstone of Newtonian physics (about a motionless body staying at rest).

How does this lead one to God? Aquinas argues as follows: If the cosmos has motion in it (and we know that it does), and if motion is always caused by something prior to it (and we know this is true as well), then there must be

23

something that started the motion in the first place—some "first mover" that was the initiator of all the motion we subsequently see. What shall we call such a first mover who initiated all of the motion in the cosmos? Aquinas says the only appropriate word is "God."

By Aquinas's own admission, this proof does not establish the existence of the *Christian* God—who parts the Red Sea, sends his son to earth, and answers prayers. But the argument does at least establish the necessity of some first and powerful entity that, itself uncaused by anything prior, initiated the motion of and in the universe. What better to label such a first entity than "God"?

This is an elegant philosophical argument and provides a model for Aquinas's other four proofs. (Check all of them out in the *Summa Theologica*, part I, question 2, article 3.) But does the argument work? It depends upon whom you ask. Throughout the Middle Ages, Aquinas's proofs were considered to be conclusive evidence of God's existence. It was not just that people believed in God (though they certainly did); it was that people believed one had to be rationally deficient—intellectually impaired—*not* to so believe. With the advent of the Enlightenment, however, philosophers began to question the soundness of Aquinas's proofs. One of the most famous critics was the great eighteenth-century philosopher Immanuel Kant (1724–1804), a believing Christian who nonetheless held that the "first mover" argument fails utterly as a logical proof. In essence, Kant suggested that Aquinas, while right in his empirical observations about motion and its causes, was wrong to posit a first mover from these observations. What Aquinas (and we) see in the physical realm is that each and every time a thing moves, it must have a mover. What Aquinas concludes at the end of his proof is that there must be a first mover,

God, that itself has motion but is unmoved by anything prior. Aquinas's conclusion, suggested Kant, directly contradicts the very empirical evidence that generates the proof in the first place, namely, that all motion is caused. God is introduced by Aquinas as an entity that defies all of the experiences of motion that we ever have had. How, Kant asks, can this be rationally justified? (See Kant's *Critique of Pure Reason*, though the work is most definitely not for the philosophically faint of heart.)

Other philosophers have come to Aquinas's defense. The French philosopher Etienne Gilson argues that while our *senses* and *reason* do not demand that we posit a first mover, our *intellect* does.[6] Again to use the pool table analogy: If the eight ball is in motion and we ask what caused it to move, we might well accept the response, "The seven ball." And if we then ask what caused the seven ball to move, we might accept the response, "The six ball." But at some point, the shrewd inquirer will demand a more definitive answer: "Hank, using a pool cue, hit the cue ball, which then hit the six ball, which then hit the seven ball, which then . . ." Indeed, for many observers, we have not really explained why the eight ball was moving in the first place until we get to Hank and his cue stick. Gilson points out that it is the *rational* (in the sense of "sensory" or "empirical") side of our human abilities that observes the eight ball moving, determines that the seven ball caused the motion, and so forth. It is our *intellect*—that intuitive faculty discussed previously in this chapter—that says, "This only makes sense as an explanation of the motion if we get to the person with the cue stick." There must be some cause of the motion in the first place.

Gilson thinks that Aquinas makes just this argument in his first mover proof. After observing a sequence of motion like the example described above, Aquinas writes, "But this cannot go on for infinity, because there would be no first mover, and consequently no other mover, seeing as the subsequent movers move only inasmuch as they are moved by the first mover. Therefore it is necessary to arrive at a first mover, moved by no other. And this everyone understands to be God."[7]

Aquinas was overly optimistic. Not *everyone* understands such a first mover to be God, at least not today. Much of modern science holds that the "thing" which initiated the

...STARRING
THE FIRST MOVER
AS MOTHER NATURE!

process of the formation of the cosmos (and the movement therein) was simply "nature." But Aquinas leaves us with an interesting question for the modern scientist: How does "nature" in this sense differ from the "God" of the religious believer? What do we mean by "God" other than, in the first instance, that force which generated the cosmos? Aquinas's proof also leaves us, along with every student who is first exposed to the big bang theory, to ask the scientist, "Yes, but who or what caused the big bang? Where did the matter that exploded come from in the first place?"

Those of you who are dissatisfied with the response "It just was" likely will find something appealing about Aquinas's first mover argument. For you, as for Aquinas, the intellect demands that there must be some start or starter—some entity wielding a giant cue stick in the sky.

Interestingly, Aquinas thought that reason could not only prove God's existence but could also tell us at least some things about the very nature of God. For instance, Aquinas argued that God must be "immutable" (i.e., unchangeable) in every way. (This point will have important implications for our discussion of human free will in chapter 3.) How did Aquinas come to this conclusion? Not by reading the Bible. If one reads through the Old and New Testaments, one might surmise that God goes through a number of significant changes. He seems, for instance, to judge humanity harshly at the time of the flood and then to treat it with forgiveness on the cross. Aquinas argues that this is incorrect. God has never changed in any way. How do we know this? By reason. If God had changed, Aquinas tells us, it could only be for better or for worse. If God is perfect, he could not have changed for the better or he would not have been perfect. He could not have changed for the worse, or he would not now be perfect. God must then be immutable.

There are problems with this argument. (Is it true that all change must be either for the better or for the worse? Could not a change be morally neutral, the equivalent of someone changing hair color from blond to brunet?) But the fact that so many modern Christians hold that God is totally changeless (especially in the face of what might be considered contrary evidence in the Bible) is testimony to the profound impact that Aquinas's new methodology had on the history of Christianity. Reason is not to be excluded from Christianity. It is the tool God has equipped us with

for understanding ourselves, the physical world around us, and even God himself. What we know and say about God should be reasonable since God is the author of a reasonable universe.

Plug this assumption into Christianity on a consistent basis, and the religion evolves in profound (and, at times, problematic) ways. In the next chapter, we will see two important examples of how.

CHAPTER THREE

Why Is There Evil?
Do Humans Have Free Will?
(and Other Questions
You're Better Off Not Asking)

Aquinas often spent years dealing with seemingly simple questions. After centuries of the so-called Dark Ages, a time when reason and logical argumentation were suppressed (in many instances by the church itself), Aquinas believed Christians needed to make rational sense out of even their most basic beliefs. They needed to face the fundamental questions about their faith.

Here is one of the most troubling: Why is there evil in the world?

For many Christians from Aquinas's age (and our own), the answer is a simple one: Satan. God creates a world of boundless goodness, and Satan enters God's creation in Eden and corrupts it throughout history. Aquinas, of course, accepts this account as *true* (all of the Bible is true for Aquinas) but adds for himself the task of showing how it is *reasonable*. How can Christians rationally account for the existence of Satan and evil in the world? This task is not as easy to accomplish as it at first may seem.

If God is truly all-powerful (or *omnipotent*), Aquinas reasons, then surely God has the power to eliminate Satan if he so chooses. One cannot say "God cannot possibly eliminate Satan" without implying that God is limited in power. If God is all knowing (or *omniscient*), then God knows about each and every one of Satan's actions, even before they occur within our temporal schema. One cannot say that God does not know about the terrible suffering that Satan has caused in the past and will cause in the future without claiming that God is limited in his knowledge. If God is all good, then he should desire the cessation of evil and injustice. One cannot claim that God wants Satan to wreak havoc on creation, or is indifferent to Satan's doing so, without undermining God's goodness.

Why then does evil persist? Why would an all-powerful, all-knowing, all-good God make evil in the first place?

These are age-old questions, and Aquinas turns to some centuries-old thinkers—most notably the ancient Greek philosopher Plato (born c. 428 B.C.) and the early church father Augustine (born A.D. 354)—for guidance.[1]

Why would God make evil in the first place? Aquinas

responds that God does *not* make evil. God only makes good. Evil, in a sense, does not exist at all—at least it is not a substance or a thing. What then is evil? It is nothing more than a "privation of the good," that is, a removal of some of the good from a good object.

An example may help here. Imagine a daisy at the peak of its beauty. Its petals are white, its center is bright yellow, and its stem is firm and green. Aquinas would say the "matter" that makes up this daisy (we might say "molecules" today) is wholly good. There is no evil substance present, only good.

Now revisit the daisy a few days later. A few petals have begun to turn brown around the edges; a leaf has dropped. We might well say that the daisy is not as good as it was a few days earlier. But what has effected this change? Not, Aquinas answers, the addition of any bad matter to the daisy. No, what caused its decline was the dissipation of some of the good that was the daisy at its height.

Come back a week later. All of the petals have dropped. The stem, once turgid, is limp and brown. The daisy's beauty is gone. Yet no badness has been added, Aquinas again points out. Rather, even more of the original good matter has dissipated. We have gone from a perfect daisy to a bad daisy without ever bringing an evil substance into the

picture. All we have observed is the continuous and gradual removal of some of the good that had previously characterized the flower.

Aquinas's surprising claim is that *all* of what we as humans call evil is like this. Evil is never a thing. It is a privation of some of the good from a wholly good substance.

What is Aquinas's goal here? Why does he introduce this rather strange argument? In simplest terms, it's to get God off the hook for creating evil. If the all-powerful, creator God sits in heaven and makes evil matter and infects the world with it, Aquinas reasons, then the problem of evil is irresolvable. If there is but one creator of everything and if anything in the world—whether a daisy or Satan— is evil in its very created substance, then the creator must be the source of evil. There can be no other reasonable conclusion.

Some groups, like the heretical Manichees (a group of self-professed Christians who accepted the teachings of a third-century Persian by the name of Mani), respond to this challenge by suggesting that God is *not* the only creator. Satan and God are cocreators. Evil exists as a substance, and Satan is the source of it.

But this view raises Satan up to a status equal to that of God. Aquinas finds this utterly unacceptable and, following Augustine, suggests a very different argument. Aquinas replies (to paraphrase), "*Neither* God *nor* Satan creates evil. There is no evil substance in the world; only good. Admittedly, at times some of the good dissipates from an object, and we humans tend to call that evil, but in point of fact, no evil exists materially. There is only good."

This may seem implausible as an explanation for our overall experience of evil. Sure, you might say, this may account for how a daisy loses its beauty, but does it account for something—or someone—like Adolf Hitler? Here, the argument goes, is the very embodiment of evil. Is Aquinas going to tell us that Hitler is wholly good but has merely had some of his goodness removed?

Aquinas's response is, in a word, yes. Hitler is no different from a daisy. (When was the last time you saw that combination of words strung end to end?) He is in substance wholly good (if not "perfectly and immutably" so; I'll say more about this strange phrase in a moment). He is created with a keen intellect and able brain, a strong heart, muscles for mobility, and a voice for oration. All of the created substance of Hitler is good. Yet when some of the good is removed from this wholly good creation (for instance, his self-control or his love of neighbor is removed) then he uses these good, created talents, such as intelligence, strength, and persuasion, for evil ends—to conquer nations, kill innocents, and so on. Has God *made* evil in creating Hitler? Not materially, replies Aquinas. God makes only good. Does Hitler *do* evil? Most certainly.

And this is just how Aquinas attempts to leave it. God never makes evil. He does make wholly good substances like people that, at times (all right, darn often), end up doing evil. Aquinas thus tries to reconcile two basic but, in some ways, seemingly conflicting Christian beliefs: God and his creation are wholly good, and the world has evil in it.

In fact, Aquinas explains Satan's existence in much the same way that I have just accounted for Hitler's. You have likely heard the claim that Satan is a "fallen angel." In Aquinas's account, you can begin to see the logic of this claim. God made Satan wholly good. He made an angel with great ability and power, an entity (like all angels) of pure, unbounded intellect. These created attributes were wholly good (but not perfectly and immutably so). When this angel rebelled against God, he did not become evil in

substance. Satan's angelic abilities are still in place and are good. But Satan has come to use these potent, created attributes for evil ends—to challenge God, to tempt creation, and so on. In a very real sense, then, for Aquinas, Satan is wholly good. This is, admittedly, a strange claim. But recognize that Aquinas intends the statement in only a formal sense. (Satan's created nature is good; his actions are not.) Besides, reasons Aquinas, such a conclusion is not only consistent with but dictated by the biblical claim in Genesis that God made the world "and it was very good." There are no exceptions—not for daisies, Hitler, or Satan.

I hope by now that you can begin to see some of the logic of Aquinas's arguments on evil. (I also hope that now you can appreciate how complicated it quickly gets for Aquinas when he attempts to prove even the most basic of

Christian beliefs by means of reason.) But if you've been following the argument carefully, you doubtlessly have begun to have some questions. I've talked about the beauty dissipating from a daisy and about some of the good being removed from Hitler or Satan but left unanswered a crucial question: Who or what causes this removal? What is the source of what Aquinas calls the "privation of the good"?

After all, if God were the one who causes the good to be removed from an angel, and that angel then becomes Satan, is not God really responsible for evil in the end? Isn't God back *on* the hook?

Aquinas, like many Christians, has difficulty with this question. As we've seen above, Aquinas does suggest that if God were to make the created world good, it had to be less than "perfectly and immutably so." In other words, it had to be made good but imperfect. Why? Well, there is only one thing that is perfectly and immutably good, and that is God himself. If the created world were created perfectly and immutably good, God would merely be producing more of himself—and that is nonsensical. Indeed, for Aquinas, *anything* created is by definition limited, if only by the simple fact that it owes its existence to something else, namely, that which created it. No, the wholly good matter that constitutes the world has to be imperfect. Hence, we must expect that good will at times decay.

But still, is not God the source of that decay (and hence the ultimate source of Satan's jealousy and Hitler's murderous acts)? Aquinas's consistency as a thinker causes him to admit that the answer is, at least in part, yes. In fact, the very "first mover" proof of God's existence that we explored in the last chapter comes back to haunt Aquinas here. In his discussion of evil, Aquinas concedes that, as first mover and first cause, God—in one important sense— *is* the cause of all things that subsequently happen, even evil.[2] If God had not initiated motion, then the motion that was Satan's entry into the garden (or Hitler's entry into Poland) would never and could never have occurred.

I admire Aquinas for this concession. Many lesser thinkers merely ignore their earlier arguments when the claims later prove inconvenient. What Aquinas will need to argue, of course, is that while God (in one formal sense) is the cause of all things that happen, he is not morally responsible for the evil acts of humans and (fallen) angels. Can this narrow line be walked?

To answer this question, we need to move from the issue that we have been exploring for the last few pages and turn to a second major example of the way in which the demand

for reasonable explanation can complicate even very simple beliefs. We need to turn from the question, "Why is there evil?" to the question, "Do humans (and angels) have free choice?"

Intuitively, the answer to this new question seems obvious: Of course we do. For instance, you can put this book down right now if you wish, without ever reading another line. Ah, you decided not to (and for that my fragile ego as an author is deeply grateful) but you *could* have stopped reading. It was *your* decision. That much is plain.

Or is it?

Some thinkers suggest that there exists a problem in believing in free choice, at least for Christians. Assume for a moment what most Christians assume: that God exists and that he is all-knowing (or *omniscient*), knowing perfectly everything that happens even before it happens. God knew when and where you would be born. God knew you would not put this book down and stop reading a moment ago. God even knew beforehand that the Lisa Marie Presley–Michael Jackson thing would never work out. (All right, maybe some things *don't* take divine omniscience to know in advance.)

What's the problem? Medieval thinkers began to wonder if there could be true human free choice in the face of a God who possessed such omniscience. Think about it for a moment. If God knew before you were ever born that on this day and at this moment you would continue to read this book, could you really have *not* continued to read it? Did you have the freedom to stop? An all-knowing God

cannot be wrong or he would not be all-knowing. If he knew you would keep reading and you had stopped, God would have known wrongly. You *had* to keep reading, no doubt about it. And if that's the case, what freedom did you have? The problem is a sticky one.

As philosophers ask, is divine omniscience consistent with human free choice? (Tip: Try this last question as an icebreaker at a party sometime. Resolve yourself to having no friends.)

Later Christians such as Martin Luther (born A.D. 1483) and John Calvin (born A.D. 1509), two of the most influential figures in Protestantism, gave up on finding a way to resolve the tension between free choice and God's knowledge. They couldn't imagine God was less than all-knowing or that he could be wrong, so they concluded that humans must not have free choice. Listen to the words of Luther (from a piece he tellingly entitled "The Bondage of the Will"): "For if we believe it to be true that God foreknows and foreordains all things; that He cannot be deceived or obstructed in His foreknowledge . . . and that nothing happens but at His will (which reason is compelled to grant); then on reason's own testimony, there can be no free will in man, or angel, or in any creature."[3] This same logic is the source of Calvin's famous concept of predestination; you are predestined by God to make the choices that you do. You have no free will.

Aquinas would have none of that. In fact, he thought he *could* have none of that. If we lack true freedom and all is predestined by God, Aquinas reasoned, how could God be just? God punishes some with eternal damnation and rewards others with salvation. If we have no free choice— if everything we do is a product of God's control—then God is unjust, punishing some poor wretches for actions that are not their own. It is as if a traffic court judge were to determine your accident was totally beyond your control and then threw you in jail regardless.

Because of this predicament, Aquinas struggled throughout his life to find a way for God to be all-powerful and all-knowing *and* for humans still to have genuine free choice. Some critics (Luther and Calvin among them) say his arguments fail. You should judge for yourself.

One attempt Aquinas makes to deal with the problem is to argue that God is *timeless*. He suggests that it is incorrect to think that God knew you would continue to read this book today *before* you actually made the choice to do so. In the *Summa*, Aquinas says that humans, living as we do *within* time, are like travelers along a road. We can see directly in front of us and a short distance behind, but uncertainty lurks beyond the next curve in the road. The future is cloudy. God, on the other hand, by knowing all perfectly, has a bird's-eye view. He sees the entire road at once—every curve and every traveler upon it. In Aquinas's words, "A man who is walking along a road cannot see those who are coming after him; but a man who looks down from a hill upon the whole length of the road can see at the same time all those who are traveling along it. So it is with God."[4] God's knowledge of time is like this bird's-eye view of the road, Aquinas says. God sees all events and all moments, in fact all of history, perfectly at once—not before they happen nor after they happen. He is *beyond time*. As such, Aquinas reasons, it is not the case that God knows what you will do *before* you do it, thus leaving you no ability to choose freely. You exist within time. God is timeless.

Is this all just fancy footwork? Is Aquinas trying to solve the problem of free choice by clever but empty wordplay? That's what his critics say, and they may have a point. After all, even if God exists outside of time, *we* exist within it,

and we are the ones whose ability to choose freely is in question.

But Aquinas offers another argument, and it's an interesting one. He claims that God can desire things to happen in two very different ways. The actual words Aquinas uses is that God wills some things to happen *necessarily* and other things to happen *contingently*. What does he mean? In effect, Aquinas tells us that God can wish for things to happen—God can create things—in two different manners.[5]

God creates some things by willing them to happen necessarily. An example would be God's announcing "Let there be light" at the beginning of the book of Genesis. Aquinas says that God willed necessarily that this light exist. As a result, there was no possibility that there would not be light. The mere fact that God willed it in this way meant that it would definitely happen. Simple enough.

Aquinas's more original idea is to say God wills other things to happen in an entirely different way: contingently. Contingent means for something to depend upon something else. What does it mean for God to will something to happen contingently?

An example might help. Imagine that God is a great lover of the game of *Monopoly*. He gathers the angels around and plays by the hour. (Somehow it makes sense

"LET'S PUT A LITTLE LIGHT ON CREATION."

that the omnipotent God would gravitate toward a game called *Monopoly*.) One night, he reaches a crucial juncture in the game and needs to roll double sixes to win (something having to do with Baltic Avenue, I'm told). Well, being God, he *could* will to roll the double sixes in the first sense discussed above. If he did so, the double sixes would definitely come up, the game would be over, and some angels might be a bit peeved. (I'm not suggesting that this was the source of the original rebellion by Satan against God, but have your ever seen the two playing *Monopoly* since?) But doing so hardly seems fair. Moreover, if God truly loves playing *Monopoly,* it's self-defeating. He would only enjoy the experience of playing the game, and potentially winning, if he had a chance to lose, to *not* roll double sixes.

Aquinas says that in such circumstances, God must have the ability to will that the double sixes come up contingently. Being a pretty smart guy, God surely knows that he needs double sixes to win. He could even wish for the double sixes to come up. But, Aquinas asks, what if God wishes for this to happen *contingent* upon the natural roll of the dice? To say that God could not do this—that he could only wish for the double sixes in such a way that they come up necessarily and he could never allow the dice to roll naturally—seems to say God is less than fully powerful. It seems to say there is something God cannot do, and it is a simple act at that: rolling dice and allowing the natural probabilities to determine how they fall. Do we really want to say that God is not capable of performing an act that any one of us could perform? Aquinas thinks that this would be absurd. No, God must be able both to wish for double sixes and to allow the dice to roll naturally.

What does this have to do with the problem of whether you have free choice? Quite a bit. What if God wills certain

things about you necessarily—that you exist, that you have an intellect, that you be born in New Jersey? Well, then, these things certainly will happen. You will exist. You will have an intellect. You will be born in New Jersey. (Hey, we'll get back to the claims of God's injustice in a minute!) But what if God wills other things about you—that you choose to develop your intellect to its fullest, that you choose to be faithful and good and thus earn salvation, that you choose to move from New Jersey—contingently? Contingent on what? Aquinas responds: contingent on your free choice. God wishes for you to develop your potential, to do the good rather than evil, and to be faithful, but in a way parallel to the sense in which he wishes for double sixes

47

when playing *Monopoly*. He wants it to occur but does not *necessitate* that it occur. Does it undermine God's power to say that God wishes for certain things to occur contingent on other things? Aquinas says heavens no! It adds to God's abilities and powers. He can create in a multitude of ways. Does it then undermine your human free choice that God wishes *contingently* that you do something? Again Aquinas responds heavens no—no more than it undermines the freedom of the dice when God wishes for double sixes but allows the natural probabilities to determine the dice's roll.

So maybe this is how we should understand the acts of evil by Satan and Hitler discussed earlier. In one sense, God as first mover is the cause of their atrocious acts. Clearly, if God as creator had not made these beings in the first place, then they could not have wreaked the havoc that they did. In another sense, though, God is not at fault. He willed that Satan and Hitler use their natural talents to serve the good, but he willed this not necessarily but contingently. It was contingent upon *their* free will. Hence, in another sense, Satan and Hitler are responsible for the evil that they do. And if that's the case, then maybe God is not culpable

for their evil acts (although he's still not off the hook for creating New Jersey).

If you followed these arguments, you're doing very well. Even professional philosophers struggle to make sense of Aquinas at times. These are some of his more difficult concepts. But they show how even very simple beliefs—in this case, the beliefs that God is all-knowing and that you have free will—can lead to sticky and complex theological issues when reason is demanded.

The nature of God, the proofs of God's existence, the problem of evil, the problem of free will—these are some of the most important theological issues, and Aquinas's responses shaped generations of Christians. Even today, one cannot pick up a book on the philosophy of religion without reading about the "first mover" argument or the idea that evil is a "privation of the good."

But it does a disservice to the legacy of Thomas Aquinas if we merely point out that he shaped theological debate. The fact of the matter is that Aquinas's application of reason as a test of existing belief eventually would become the standard of truth not merely for Christians but for much of the world. And his ideas on some topics would come to shape not only Christian belief but also the mainstream intellectual traditions of the West. All of us—Christian and non-Christian alike—are in some sense Thomists. In the coming chapters, we'll see how by exploring some of Aquinas's influential contributions to important practical areas of inquiry such as law, morality, women, and politics.

Our first stop, though, is a topic that is anything but practical, though it is essential to our understanding of what is to come. The topic is one crucial to Aquinas but rarely discussed today: metaphysics. Brace yourself.

CHAPTER FOUR

Metaphysics 101
(or Why We Are What We Are)

Ranking high on the top ten list of "All-Time Great Conversation Stoppers" (alongside "Have you heard about my battle with gout" and "Hey, can you pluck this for me") is the phrase, "Let's talk about metaphysics." It is a strange topic, abstract and at times off-putting. The prefix *meta* is from the Greek, roughly translated as "after." So *meta*-physics is the study of that which is after or beyond the physical realm (and is contrasted with physics, which, of course, concentrates on the physical realm).

While today most people use the term to refer to things like the inquiry into ghosts or the spirit realm, for Aquinas metaphysics has far broader meaning. Aquinas defines metaphysics as "the science of being." It is, he tells us, the inquiry into the very essence of an object—the study of what makes a thing a thing.

Uh-oh. I can sense your eyes glazing over already. Let me see if I can make this notion a little more accessible—and show you why you should care.

As we have already seen, philosophers like Aquinas often concern themselves with issues taken for granted by most people. (As if I had to tell you this.) The question of whether humans have free will is one example that we've already explored. Another example is found in metaphysics.

The central question that Aquinas as metaphysician is concerned with is this: What makes a thing the thing that it is? Some specific examples will help, and I'll start with a simple one.

Imagine that on the page in front of you is a big, green triangle. What is the significance of this triangle? Well, the physicist would answer this question by making inquiries about the triangle's physical nature: It is flat, it is four

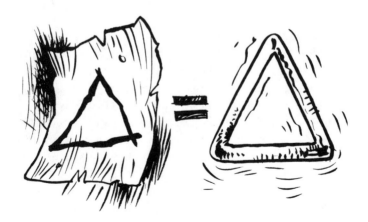

inches tall, it is green, it is made of paper. The metaphysician, on the other hand, might ask, "What conceptually makes that shape on the page in front of you a 'triangle' in the first place? What defines the object as a triangle?"

Aquinas would point out that certain characteristics about the object in front of you are inconsequential to its being a triangle: the fact that it is green, the fact that it is four inches high, the fact that it is made of paper. These are what he calls "accidents" in the metaphysical sense; they are not part of what makes the object a triangle—not part of its "essence," as Aquinas puts it. The object could be red instead of green and five inches tall instead of four, and it would still be a triangle. Well, if the color and the size are "accidental" characteristics of a triangle, then the metaphysician asks, "What are the *essential* attributes?" What makes the triangle triangular? The answer, of course, is that a triangle is a geometric figure with three sides. Change *this* characteristic—give the object four sides rather than three, for instance—and you no longer have a triangle. It is *essential* to a triangle that it have three sides.

Here's another example. What is the essence of a bachelor? A particular bachelor, Sam, may have brown hair, own a bar in Boston, and be six feet four inches tall. These are traits accidental to Sam being a bachelor. Change any or all and the person in question still could be a bachelor. What is essential to Sam being a bachelor is, of course, that he be an unmarried, adult male. Take that characteristic away—for instance, stipulate that Sam is an adult male who owns a bar in Boston and who is married—and one no longer has a bachelor.

I bet you didn't think metaphysics was so simple. Unfortunately, it's not. For (as I'm sure you already suspect), Aquinas is not concerned about defining the essence of triangles or bachelors (as much fun as this can be). He is

concerned with far more difficult undertakings. What is the essence of God? Of an angel? Of a human being? Of a law? What specifically makes each of these incredibly complex entities, with thousands of discernable characteristics, the thing that it is? Which characteristics are essential? Which are accidental?

In small ways, we've already been engaged in doing metaphysics in this volume. (I'm one sneaky guy.) For example, earlier we asked, in effect, is it essential to God that he be immutable? Could God change and still be God? (Aquinas's response was that, no, he could not.) We have also seen Aquinas argue that it is part of his essence that God be omnipotent, omniscient, and all-good. Take any one of these characteristics away and you no longer have God (at least according to Aquinas). We also have seen Aquinas say of angels and humans that it is *not* part of their essence that they do evil. Satan and Hitler may choose to engage in evil acts, but, Aquinas tells us, doing so is not part of their created essences. Evil is thus accidental to the natures of humans and angels. In fact, in the *Summa Theologica* Aquinas actually argues that all evil is an accident.[1] This claim, as you can imagine, is often misunderstood by modern readers. It is not that Aquinas is saying that God somehow slipped up and, oops, accidentally made evil. Rather, his claim is a metaphysical one. Evil is not essential to any created object—Adam, for example—any more than being green is essential to a triangle or being tall is essential to being a bachelor. Individual triangles may be green, individual bachelors may be tall, and, yes, Adam may do evil, but none of these things is essential to the very metaphysical nature of the object in question. This adds another facet to Aquinas's response to the problem of evil. Evil does exist in the cosmos, but not as part of the essence of the created realm—not as part of what God intentionally and purposefully creates. Thus, God is once again separated (to a degree) from the creation of evil.

If evil is not part of the nature of any object in creation, what is? This is a highly important question since its answer will have a profound impact on what Aquinas says about law, morality, and politics. What is the metaphysical essence of the objects of creation?

Aquinas argues that one crucial way of establishing the nature of an object is to determine its end or goal. If we are to determine that person A is an airline pilot and person B is a baker, it will be (in large part) because we first establish that person A sets out to direct planes to their appropriate destination while person B sets out to produce breads and pastries. It is their end or goal that establishes what they are.

The same is true of all objects, Aquinas tells us. What an object is, is (largely) determined by its end. The end is the starting point for determining the essence of an object. Simple enough.

So what is the end of created objects? Aquinas's answer is controversial and surprising. Aquinas says that all objects share one end in common, and that end is the ultimate good, namely, God. All things naturally—by their very created nature—seek God. As we will see, Aquinas holds that this is certainly true of intellectual beings like people and angels. But it is also true of nonintellectual entities like trees and lions, and even of inanimate objects like rocks. What Aquinas is saying is that in each case the entity has as part of its very nature the end or goal of serving God. When a mountain lion kills a deer, it is serving God's plan by sustaining the species of lions and by winnowing out the deer population—hence, protecting the balance of the ecosystem. When a tree grows toward the heavens, it serves God by providing fruits and nuts for other creatures, by processing the constituents of air through photosynthesis, and by providing wood so that humans might build

houses. When a rock . . . well, sits there, it provides shelter for bugs and shade for snakes. The ultimate end of each of these entities is to serve God—and his plan for the cosmos—in however small a way.

Of course, animals and trees serve God "naturally." Because they lack the human faculty of free choice, lions instinctively act in ways that serve God and his purposes; trees do so inevitably by means of their created nature. Each fulfills its metaphysical end by necessity. Humans are another matter entirely.

According to Aquinas, humans are created in such a way that we only fulfill our nature when we seek and serve God.[2] But because we are creatures of free choice (see the discussion in chapter 3), we (along with the angels) have

the unique ability *not* to fulfill our created end if we so choose. The tree naturally grows toward the heavens. The lion instinctively hunts the deer. But not all humans act in ways that serve and seek God. True, Aquinas tells us, we are only truly fulfilled when we do so (since it is part of our metaphysical nature or essence). But does this mean that we always seek God? Far from it. It does mean, though, that when we fail to do so, we inevitably fail to find happiness and completeness as human beings. In effect, we are denying our nature.

An analogy may help here. As human beings, we all have certain common nutritional needs. We need a certain amount of vitamin C, protein, and so forth or we do not flourish. (Indeed, we may not even survive.) As creatures with free choice, we could deny these nutritional needs. You could wake up tomorrow and vow never to drink another glass of orange juice or consume another ounce of protein. Instead, you will merely consume typing paper: three sheets of paper, three meals a day. (Believe me, in writing this book, the thought has crossed my mind!) The fact that you make such a choice, however, does not change the basic fact that you need vitamin C and protein to survive. This is a fact no amount of willing could ever change. Why? Because these nutritional requirements are

part of your very created nature; they are part of your essence.

The same is true, Aquinas says, of the end that we have as human beings to seek God. You can, by your free choice, deny that God is important to you. You can become a rabid atheist and seek satisfaction in secular matters alone— trying to find fulfillment exclusively in peanut butter cups and Britney Spears videos (but enough about me). But, and here's the controversial point, Aquinas says that you'll never be really happy, you'll never be fulfilled. (Apparently, Aquinas never saw a Britney Spears video.) Like the person who eats typing paper, the person who tries to exist with-

TRIANGLES ARE QUITE USEFUL, ACTUALLY, TO THE FIRST MOVER!

out seeking God is acting in denial of her basic human nature. It is part of the metaphysical essence of human beings to seek God.

It is a crucial tenet of Aquinas's metaphysics—indeed, of his entire philosophical system—that all things by their nature seek the good, which is God. This is not to say that all things always act in ways consistent with this end. It is to say, though, that they *should*.

This controversial metaphysical assumption sits at the very foundation of one of Aquinas's most important con-tributions to the modern world—his views on law and morality.

CHAPTER FIVE

Law and Morality

Men can fashion patterns of thought, but God himself arranged the natural order.

Thomas Aquinas

If you've followed the discussion of metaphysics in the previous chapter, you (perhaps without knowing it) have acquired the basic pieces necessary to understand Aquinas's highly influential views on morality and the law. To see how, we'll have to turn to the section of the *Summa* in which he discusses the various types of law.[1]

According to Aquinas, "The whole community of the Universe is governed by divine reason."[2] What he means is that everything that exists—from the movement of planets to the interaction of atoms—acts according to a plan set forth by God. The all-powerful, all-knowing, all-good God leaves no detail unattended. Each and every thing has a purpose, an "end" as we discussed in chapter 4. It is not, for instance, that God has a purpose for human beings but not for fleas, for angels but not for grains of sand. *All* created things act according to a plan

devised by God. This all-encompassing plan is what Aquinas calls "the eternal law."

In modern times, when we use the word "law" we can mean one of (at least) two very different things. At times we are referring to things such as the law of gravity or the second law of thermodynamics—so-called scientific laws. At other times we are referring to things such as the Ten Commandments or the Golden Rule, what might be called "moral laws." It is important to understand that, for Aquinas, the eternal law includes *both* of these types of laws (and a great deal more). All of the intricacies of the cosmos are included.

Of course, to know the details of God's infinitely complex scheme for the universe is something that is possible for God alone. One would have to be perfectly knowing to grasp the purpose and plan for every atom, for every grain of sand. No human, no matter how bright, could ever understand the whole of the eternal law. (Even that Eddie dog on *Frasier* would probably have a hard time.) Besides, reasons Aquinas, a law is only binding on an entity when the law is made known to that object. A legislature that passes a new traffic law, for example, but never makes the law public cannot expect people to follow the new rule. This leads Aquinas to discuss a second, and all-important, aspect of the law. That subset of the infinitely detailed eternal law that can be known by means of reason—and hence that can be known to (and binding upon) humans—is what Aquinas calls the "natural law."

Of all the components of the eternal law, Aquinas discusses the natural law almost exclusively. This is only fitting since, by definition, humans can have nothing to say about the other aspects of the eternal law. We will never grasp the vast majority of their details—human reason is simply inadequate—so why waste time trying? (An interesting aside:

One of the gifts that God bestows upon blessed humans upon their deaths is the ability to see the whole of the eternal law. This is the beatific vision—but even then it comes to us not via reason but by means of the revelation of God.) What *is* worth our time—and crucial to the health and survival of the human species—is to uncover those aspects of the eternal law that we *can* know. When scientists apply their reason to discover physical aspects of the eternal law, we end up with the laws of science. When theologians and philosophers apply their reason to issues of right and wrong—to questions of human behavior—we end up with the moral law.

In many ways, according to Aquinas, doing morality differs little from doing metaphysics. As we've seen, the task of metaphysics is to determine the essence of a thing. Morality also is concerned with discovering this essence and simply adds this: Since God is the source of the essence of all things, one morally must pursue those actions that promote and avoid those actions that oppose an entity's essence. For example, if it truly is part of what makes a mountain lion a mountain lion that it hunt deer, then for humans to do things that make it impossible for mountain lions to hunt their prey would be "wrong"; such actions would be opposed to God and his plan of creation. If it is truly part of our physiological makeup as humans that we require sixty milligrams of vitamin C a day, then to act in ways that allow for people to satisfy this requirement would be "right" or "good." The moral good becomes, quite simply, that which is in accord with the order created by

God (and hence in accord with reason); the moral evil becomes that which opposes this order.

In this simple idea is evidenced another great contribution that Aquinas makes to the shift from the Dark Ages to the Renaissance and eventually the Enlightenment. Sure, moral truths are contained in the Bible, Aquinas tells us. One can and should consult the Bible for the Ten Commandments and for important dictates about loving one's neighbor, turning the other cheek, and so forth. But one can also find these (and other) moral truths by an alternate route: reason. If one, by means of reason, taps into and conforms to the natural law of God, one is morally in the right. If one acts contrary to reason and hence against the natural law of God, one is morally wrong.

In fact, according to Aquinas, both of the two central intellectual faculties possessed by humans that we discussed in chapter 2—intellect and reason—are necessary to this process of pursuing the moral good. The *intellect,* the intuitive faculty drawn to nonempirical truths, discovers the proper *end* in a given situation. For instance, the intellect provides the individual with the knowledge that "good is to be done and promoted, and evil is to be avoided." This is a so-called first principle—an "ought"—which cannot itself be established by empirical evidence. *Reason,* the faculty that processes sensory or empirical data, then steps in, and by means of an analysis of practical experience tells us the best *means* for arriving at the end in question.[3] It might be that when we examine the results of specific instances of lying, for example, the good is not promoted. Reason determines that lying is a poor means to the good.

Here's an example that Aquinas himself offers. One central truth of Aquinas's morality (and one central to his political views as well) is that human beings only fully flourish when they live in community and that such flourishing is a good thing that should be pursued. How do we know this to be true? By a combination of both intellect and reason. It takes the intuitive faculty of the intellect to make the judgment that a person immersed in the language, commerce, and human exchange of social life lives a "better" form of existence than does the hermit. This is a value judgment that no amount of empirical evidence alone can establish. Once this fact is established—and with it, an end or goal that should be pursued—the moral question becomes: By what means can humans best pursue this goal of living in society? Here the empirical faculty, reason, kicks it. It looks out into the world, analyzes different responses to this question and their results, and determines the best course or *means* to the end. It looks at Dennis Rodman's approach to living and working with others in the community that is a basketball team, for instance, and compares it with Michael Jordan's. It examines how petulance and self-promotion, on the one hand, and cooperation and self-sacrifice, on the other, serve to contribute to or detract from the social good. The result, if one makes use of reason well, are ethical conclusions that are part of the natural law. Thus, to avoid needlessly offending those among whom one has to live becomes one simple dictate of morality, according to Aquinas. (Sorry, Dennis.) If we are to flourish in society, we should work to get along with others. This is hardly an earth-shattering moral insight, but it illustrates the important mechanism for how, according to Aquinas, reason and intellect come together to discover the natural law.

Like many of the changes that he effected in Western thought, Aquinas's description of how we go about discovering moral truth seems less than revolutionary by modern standards. It seems almost traditional. (One reason for this is that Aquinas has proven so influential in *shaping*

tradition.) After all, he is not suggesting that the findings of reason will ever contradict the moral assertions of the Bible. Just the opposite: Aquinas is confident that the Bible puts forth flawless moral truth and, as such, can never be contradicted by any moral conclusion correctly drawn by reason. The implications of Aquinas's introduction of a "natural law" to ethics, however, are far reaching.

For one thing, his natural law theory reveals a certain optimism about the human condition—an optimism that, while novel in Aquinas's day, has become a defining trait of the modern age. It is our very nature, Aquinas tells us, to pursue the good. We have good natural inclinations, and we have all kinds of God-given tools (such as reason and intellect) to help us find that good.

In contrast, for many Christians in medieval times (and today), the most prominent characteristic of human beings is their sinfulness. We are wretched and bad, and left to our own devices, we will pursue sinful acts. The highly influential church father Augustine (born A.D. 354) writes in his *Confessions*: "I have myself seen the jealousy in a baby and know what it means. He was not old enough to talk, but whenever he saw his foster-brother at the breast, he would grow pale with envy."[4] This is evidence of the sin of Adam, Augustine tells us, and it hopelessly corrupts all humans before they even emerge from the womb. This perspective convinced many Christians that their only hope was to follow the church blindly and without question.

For Aquinas, while the sin of Adam is very real, its effect is less devastating. Original sin corrupts our once pure reason so that at times we choose the wrong means to the good (and hence end up doing bad). But (unlike in Augustine's account) the good is still the thing we seek. Even a "monster," Aquinas tells us, seeks good things like peace and security; he merely chooses the wrong means to those ends because of his flawed reason. That humans are good, that they can usually be trusted, and that they have both the inclination and the ability to find the truth all are ideas put forth by Aquinas that would later become hallmarks of the Enlightenment.

A second reason why Aquinas's introduction of natural law theory was so revolutionary is that it provided a common basis for all peoples to discuss moral issues. As European Christianity encountered the Muslim, Jewish, and (eventually) secular worlds, New Testament teachings no longer could be employed to settle ethical debate. Something more common, something universal, was needed. As Aquinas writes, "It follows therefore that natural law in its first common principles is the same among all men, both as to validity and recognition."[5] The natural law, "written on the hearts" of all people, provided a common language of

ethics. As we will see, it would eventually contribute greatly to the emergence of international law.

A third and related reason for the immense influence of natural law is that it gave Christians themselves the ability to comment on moral issues *not* discussed by the Bible. If one takes the approach that the only moral truths are those that are put forth explicitly in the Bible (as many contemporary Christian fundamentalists claim, for instance), then what does one do with questions about the morality of nuclear arms, artificial insemination, and cloning—all issues that are never explicitly mentioned in the Bible? Many modern Protestants, following Luther's famous dictate "Scripture alone," fall silent in the face of "new" moral issues—issues unmentioned and seemingly unanticipated by the Bible. Others are far from silent but are able to offer only questionable biblical footing for their strong opinions on these topics.

In contrast, modern Roman Catholics have for decades taken a lead among Christians in the discussion of such moral topics as medical and nuclear ethics. Why? In a word: Aquinas. By introducing reason as an alternative path to the moral truth, Aquinas supplied Catholic Christians with a means of addressing issues not considered by the Bible.

One example is environmental issues. While the Bible talks about the relationship between human beings and God's creation in general terms, during biblical times there was little awareness of the environmental challenges that we face in the twenty-first century. Animals were to be hunted, nature was to be "subdued," and there was no thought that these things could be hunted and subdued into extinction. Aquinas's natural law approach to morality, in contrast, has profound implications for human interaction with the environment today. If the point of ethics in general is to discover

the essence of each aspect of creation—humans, lions, fish, trees, and so forth—and then to pursue actions that promote the flourishing of that essence, Aquinas (and his natural law approach) could be seen as a philosophical ancestor to the modern "green movement." If it is part of the lion's essence to hunt antelope on the plains, then one had better not destroy the lion's habitat. To do so would be a violation of the natural law and of God. If it is part of the essence of salmon to spawn, thus providing food for grizzlies and other creatures in the Pacific Northwest, then we as humans have a moral obligation to protect this process. Of course, it should also be pointed out, lest you think he was a card-carrying member of PETA, that Aquinas held that part of the God-created purpose of many animals was to serve as food for humans. As a result, hunting becomes a definite good, at least by Aquinas's own application of his natural law. But even here there are limits: Hunting is consistent with the natural law when one uses the prey for food or some other good; hunting is not necessarily a good when engaged in for sport (i.e., for the sake of pure entertainment).

Aquinas, of course, never explicitly developed his natural law stance into a full-fledged environmental theory able to deal with the range of modern questions that we now face. That, of course, is precisely my point. Natural law provides a moral approach with enough flexibility to deal with new issues as they emerge.

This is not only true of animal rights but of human rights. Some of the most revolutionary words in history were: "We hold these truths to be self-evident, that all men are created equal." When Thomas Jefferson wrote this famous opening to the Declaration of Independence, he was explicitly appealing to the natural law tradition that Aquinas was so instrumental in bringing to prominence. Jefferson's complaint about King George's taxation of the colonists was not an objection to written law codes (the so-called positive law). The British could point to written laws that said they had the right to tax the colonists. No, Jefferson's appeal was to a law written not in code books or even in the Bible but "on the hearts of men"—in their reason. His appeal, quite explicitly, was to the natural law. Today, the natural law is the basis for not merely the moral principles at the foundation of the American form of government, but also for such modern moral documents as the United Nations' Declaration of Human Rights, the Nuremberg War-Crimes Codes, and the Geneva Convention. In each case, the document appeals not to religious texts but to a moral law that, it is claimed, is universally accessible to all people via their reason and must never be violated. In each case, the codes appeal to something very much like Aquinas's concept of natural law.

In the coming chapters, we'll take a look at how Aquinas's natural law approach has shaped our modern attitudes about some of the most important moral issues: sexuality, war, gender, and politics.

CHAPTER SIX

The Ins and Outs of Sex

One of the most fascinating—and influential—examples of Aquinas's use of natural law to establish what he believes to be moral truths is his discussion of human sexuality. It is not an overstatement to say that Aquinas has influenced modern Western conceptions of sexuality more than any figure other than Augustine. (Yes, even more than Madonna.) There is some irony here. As we saw at the beginning of our discussion, in his entire life Aquinas never engaged in sex. Yet his views still define much of the debate today. (Those who can, do; those who can't, teach?)

In trying to determine what God's "natural law" has to say about sex, Aquinas first asks what is the end of sex, what is its purpose? For an answer, we *could* consult the Bible: "Be fruitful and multiply" (Gen. 1:28). But what does this mean exactly? Do we always have to "be fruitful"—seek procreation—in each and every sex act? Can we be celibate and still be true to the Bible? How? Is birth control acceptable? What about in vitro fertilization? Fortunately, Aquinas thinks, we have additional resources at our disposal for answering such questions. We can find God's plan for sexuality by means of our reason. We can use the intellectual faculties with which God has supplied us and ask, "Why sex?"

For Aquinas, reason comes back with a threefold answer to this important question. First, sex is for the purpose of procreation. Our reason reveals to us that when a man and a woman join in the sexual act, they physiologically "fit" together, and the coupling results in the potential production of offspring. Surely, Aquinas reasoned, this was not an accident but God's very intent in creating sexuality. Procreation is part of the *essence* of sexuality. For some Christian figures, Augustine among them, this procreative end was the *only* godly purpose of sex. Aquinas disagrees. He argues that any rational observer of the sex act (I'm not implying here that Aquinas was a voyeur) would have to concede that a second purpose of sex is to bind a husband and wife together in unity. Sex not only holds the potential for producing offspring; it also can serve to bring two people closer to each other in the bond of love. Is not this also part of God's plan in creating sex—is it not part of sex's *essence*—asks Aquinas? That is not all. There is yet another created end to sex according to Aquinas. Sex not only preserves the species and strengthens marriage, it provides great pleasure to the participants. This pleasure too, then, is part of God's divine plan.

These claims may seem obvious to a modern reader, but

they were radical at the time. The highly influential Augustine earlier had established the leading Christian understanding of sex accepted during Aquinas's day. In his great work *The City of God*, Augustine argued that before the fall in the garden of Eden, sex had been a purely rational undertaking—no different from taking a drink of water.[1] Both were activities needed for the survival of the individual/species. Both were performed matter-of-factly. When the human species needed to reproduce, the male would command, "Penis arise" (I think I saw David Copperfield

perform this trick once at the Mirage in Vegas), and he then would perform a rational, clinical act of reproduction with his partner. It is only with the fall that passion and pleasure enter the sex act, according to Augustine.

Unfortunately, humans sinned so quickly that Adam and Eve never got a chance to try out sex in its passionless form. (Passionless sex would only come later. We now call it "marriage.") As punishment for his disobedience to God, Adam's sexual organs were taken out of his rational control and subjected to the whims of the passions. (A rough translation of Augustine's own words from *The City of God* about his member is "It has a mind of its own.") Sex acts, as a result, become infected by sin and turn into acts of self-love, that is, people desire sex not to reproduce but to satisfy their own selfish desires. In fact, Augustine tells us, sex—and more particularly, the male semen—actually becomes the conduit for the passage of original sin from one generation to the next. (This is why Jesus is born of woman but not of man. For Jesus to have been born untainted by original sin, Augustine reasons, he *had* to have been conceived without semen.) Such is the wretched legacy of Adam and Eve—and the insidious role pleasure now plays in the sex act—according to Augustine.

Nonsense, responds Aquinas. It is clear that pleasure is part of the designed purpose of the sex act, a purpose provided for by *God*. There is no sin in partaking in this pleasure—indeed, there is sin in not doing so. Seek (and impart) pleasure! It's part of God's plan for sex. He writes: "The exceeding pleasure experienced in the sex act, so long as it is in harmony with reason, does not destroy the balance of virtue."[2] This may hardly seem like a ringing endorsement, but compared to Augustine's dark portrayals it was a veritable proclamation of hedonism. The only restriction, Aquinas tells us, is that one also and simultaneously must

aim to satisfy the other designed aspects of the sex act—procreation and unity. Seek pleasure, but also seek procreation and unity with one's spouse. Pleasure becomes sinful in the sex act only when it overshadows the other designed ends of sex and becomes the exclusive purpose.

So (at least as traditional Catholicism has interpreted Aquinas) there are three rationally derived purposes of sex. But note that: one must seek all three ends in each and every sex act. This is a crucial point and, as we will see, serves to distinguish the views of Aquinas (and of Roman Catholicism in general) from those of many other Christians. The point is also central to understanding Aquinas's hugely influential views on sexual sin. Let's take a look at how.

If the natural law (in general) commands that we pursue the created essence of each thing, and sex was created with a threefold essence, then we sin anytime we deviate from the ends of sex. Moreover, Aquinas argues that we rationally can determine how serious a sexual sin is by establishing how far it deviates from those ends. A slight deviation is a slight sin; a major deviation becomes an egregious sin. In the *Summa Theologica*, Aquinas introduces a fascinating and highly influential ranking of sexual sins. Before we look at it, two caveats. First, this section has a PG-13 rating. Children under thirteen must be accompanied by a parent, guardian, or Madonna. Second, Aquinas's ranking only makes sense if we add one point that Aquinas suggests but never makes explicit. The three ends of sex that we have discussed need to be ordered in terms of importance, with conception the most important, unity between husband and wife of secondary importance, and pleasure of lesser importance. With these caveats in mind, those of you over thirteen (all right, all right, *all* of you) can proceed to Aquinas's ranking.

The least serious of the sexual sins—though a grave sin nonetheless—is *fornication* (or premarital sex, as it would be termed today) between an unmarried man and an unmarried woman. Why is this a sin? Pleasure is sought. So too *could* procreation be. (We'll get to the case of the unmarried—and married—couples that use birth control in a minute.) The problem with fornication is that it does not satisfy the third end of sex—strengthening the marriage bond of love between the couple since, of course, the couple is not married. Because it fails to satisfy one of the three ends, fornication is a sin and must be avoided.

The next most serious sexual sin is *adultery*. Why is adultery more serious than fornication? Couples engaged in adultery certainly seek pleasure in the sex act. They could seek procreation; at least such is physically possible. But in

the case of adultery, the violation of the end of unity is even greater than in the case of fornication. In a case of adultery, at least one of the parties by definition is married to another person. The act of adultery thus not only fails to strengthen the marriage of the couple engaged in sex (since they are not married to each other), it harms the marriage bond that does exist between the adulterer and his or her spouse. Since adultery deviates further from the sexual ideal than fornication, it is the graver sin.

Even more severe a sexual sin than adultery is *rape*, since it violates two of the three ends of sex. While procreation is possible, the act of rape destroys the ends both of unity and pleasure. In the act of violence that is rape, none of the ends but (at least in theory) procreation is satisfied.

Fornication, adultery, and rape are all what Aquinas calls "sins against right reason." If you are using your reason properly, he thinks, you will know that each of these acts is to be avoided—even if one has not read about these wrongs in the Bible. These three are not, however, the worst sexual sins by Aquinas's logic. Each of the three sexual acts discussed so far at least holds the potential for procreation. Man and woman are joining together and performing sex in such a way that conception is physically possible—and this, after all, is the first and foremost purpose to sex, Aquinas reasons.

Far more serious than the "sins against right reason" are the "sins against nature": masturbation, sodomy (including homosexuality), and bestiality. Perpetrators of these acts all are guilty of a violation of sex's most important purpose—procreation.

Like the first group of sexual sins, Aquinas tells us that we can rank this second group with regard to severity. *Masturbation* is the least severe of the three. It does produce pleasure, but it cannot result in procreation and it does not provide for unity—except perhaps in the case of schizophrenics, but that's a story for another day. (Be sure to look for my groundbreaking work on the topic, "Is Unity at Hand?") Note another strange implication of Aquinas's views: Masturbation becomes a more serious sexual sin than fornication, adultery, or even rape. Why? Because both of the two most significant ends of sex—procreation and uniting husband and wife—are violated by masturbation. Only the pleasure criterion is met. The act deviates further from the essence of sex than does even rape. (To be fair, it should be pointed out that rape is not merely a sin of sex but also a sin of violence by Aquinas's account. Hence, all things considered, Aquinas would hold it is worse for one to commit rape than to engage in masturbation—even though masturbation is the more serious *sexual* sin.)

Perhaps you now can begin to see why Roman Catholics historically have been stronger opponents of masturbation than have many other Christians. The Bible says little or nothing about the topic (some people claim that the sin of Onan in Genesis 38:1–10 is a reference to the act), and many Protestant denominations today regard masturbation to be normal, even healthy. (All right, most Protestant denominations prefer not to talk about it at all, but even *that* is significant.) But official Catholic doctrine *does* talk about masturbation and, to this day, regards it to be a grave violation of the moral law. (Many is the

parochial school child who has been lectured on the dangers of the act, though few of these children, to my knowledge, *actually* have gone blind.) Aquinas was a critical figure in this history.

Today Catholics also stand in the minority among Christians in opposing the practice of artificial insemination, even in cases when the husband is the sperm donor and his own wife is the recipient. What could be the moral complaint against a procedure that gives many married couples their lone hope of conceiving a child? The short answer is: Aquinas's natural law argument. The semen for artificial insemination is produced by an act of masturbation, and the latter (as we've just seen) is a severe violation of the natural law by Catholic reckoning. With cloning a looming possibility for humans from a technological perspective, it will be interesting to see if this affects the Catholic argument against masturbation. If it only takes one human cell (and not the joining of sperm and egg) to "conceive" a new human life, could one have a procreative intent in the act of masturbation? Stay tuned.

Even more severe than masturbation as a sin against nature is *sodomy*. Sodomy, like masturbation, violates both the procreative and unitive functions of sex (satisfying only the end of pleasure)—but, unlike masturbation, sodomy involves two parties rather than one and hence is "doubly" immoral. Modern audiences may be surprised to learn that when Aquinas condemns sodomy he is not merely opposing homosexual acts. Acts of sodomy between heterosexual couples—even husband and wife— are also severely condemned. Some acts of sodomy *might* help to unite husband and wife in love (Aquinas would have had strong doubts about this claim), but none of them lead to conception. Thus, they are all serious "sins against nature."

Aquinas's natural law argument here is crucial to understanding the famous opposition by Roman Catholicism to *birth control*. Even within the bonds of marriage, using birth control is not a minor but a severe violation of the natural law according to Catholic doctrine. In fact, birth control becomes the moral equivalent of sodomy and every bit as serious a sin. We can now see why. In each case, the parties perform a sex act that intentionally violates the end of reproduction.

Of course, Aquinas's arguments here also have much to say about Roman Catholic and other modern opposition to *homosexuality*. (While Aquinas's natural law arguments on birth control have been rejected by most Protestants, for instance, his arguments about homosexuality have not.) In Aquinas's schema, all homosexual acts become "sins against nature" since none can result in conception. Aquinas also felt that such acts could not be unitive since the couple brought together was not and could not be married in the eyes of God. The only end served was pleasure.

Such depictions of homosexuality, for good or for ill, have had a lasting impact. They still shape much of the contemporary debate on the topic. How often have you heard an opponent of homosexuality condemn the act as simply "unnatural" and hence horribly wrong? To a significant degree, Aquinas is the source of this association. But surprisingly, Aquinas's arguments recently have opened the door to several *defenses* of homosexuality by modern Christian theologians.

Robert Wood, for instance, suggests that if homosexuality can be shown to be genetically determined—if homosexuality is something one is born with—then it would seem to be "natural" in the most basic sense. As part of God's created plan, it can hardly be condemned as ungodly. Wood even argues that God designed homosexuality as a natural way of keeping population size in check.[3] For those who disagree with Wood, it is important to recognize that Aquinas's traditional view—that couples must seek conception in each and every act of sex—does pose a large challenge to modern attempts to control world population growth. When a recent United Nations commission on overpopulation suggested that birth control education be a cornerstone of the commission's efforts, Roman Catholic groups played a large role in scuttling the proposal.

Perhaps even more interesting is an argument that seems wildly implausible initially but, if one accepts some of Aquinas's basic assumptions, may be legitimate: Homosexual acts *can* satisfy the procreative criteria of sex. Farfetched? Let's see. To understand the argument, let's go back to a decision made by Pope Pius XI in 1930. Pope Pius faced a difficult (and seemingly unrelated) question. If one or both members of a married couple become(s) infertile—say that the wife undergoes a radical hysterectomy after thirty years of loving devotion to her husband—does this mean that the married couple can never have sex again without violating the natural law? After all, in one sense, no sex act can be truly procreative when either of the parties is infertile. Although far from a novel problem, this challenge was becoming a more poignant and pressing one when Pius was forced to address it in 1930. Previously there had certainly been infertile couples, but there was always a great deal of uncertainty involved (i.e., Betty hasn't conceived after ten years of marriage, but might she not tomorrow?). By the 1930s, in at least some cases the mystery had been removed by modern medicine. The doctor extracting Betty's uterus is able to inform her, in no uncertain terms, that she will never bear a child again. Does sex with Betty then become the moral equivalent of an act of sodomy—one of the most serious of "sins against nature"—since it can no longer be procreative?

Pope Pius's humane answer was no. The married couple suffering from, as he put it, "certain defects" can continue to have sex without violating the natural law. How? The answer is largely a Thomistic one. The crucial consideration is whether or not the couple has a procreative *intent*—whether or not they want to reproduce. The issue is not whether they actually do so. After all, most acts of even unprotected sex between fertile, married couples do not lead to conception. Thus, the rule cannot be that every sex act has to actually lead to reproduction for it to be moral. The issue is whether or not the husband and wife *want* their sex act to result in children. (This, by the way, is one explanation for why birth control remains so problematic for many Catholic thinkers, even if it, in an individual instance, fails to prevent conception. Using birth control shows the couple most explicitly *not* to have a procreative intent.) Pope Pius's ruling thus allows for the infertile married couple to continue to engage in sex. Even the woman who has undergone a radical hysterectomy can "hope for a miracle." This seems a sensible ruling and one true to the spirit of Aquinas's argument.

What does all of this have to do with the issue of homosexuality? If the infertile couple does not violate the procreative purpose of sex as long as they "hope for a miracle" despite the physical impossibility, why cannot the homosexual couple hope for a *really* big miracle and satisfy the natural law as well? After all, many homosexual couples would love for their sex acts to be able to result in conception. How are such couples different from the infertile heterosexual couple?

It's an interesting question, and it would be fascinating to see how Aquinas would address it if he were still around. Aquinas would most certainly not adopt the knee-jerk reaction of many contemporary Christians when they are first exposed to such arguments. Aquinas would ask how one rationally can distinguish between the two cases, especially if one is committed to saying that the crucial issue is not whether one has the *ability* to conceive but the *desire* to do so. Cannot straight and gay couples alike have such a desire? If one says, on the other hand, that the issue is not about desire but ability, does that mean that infertile individuals—postmenopausal women, for instance—are guilty of a grave "sin against nature" whenever they engage in sex, even within the bonds of marriage? Is one forced to say that such individuals are morally equivalent to sodomites?

These are the interesting questions posed to us by contemporary discussions of homosexuality and the natural law.

One famous, if indirect, response was offered by Pope Paul VI in his encyclical on the regulation of birth, *Humanae Vitae* (1968). In what was viewed by some observers to be a significant break with Catholic tradition, Pope Paul argued that a procreative intent is not necessary in each and every sex act within the bonds of marriage. With "natural family planning," also known as the "rhythm method"—a process by which the couple intentionally engages in intercourse only during those times of the month in which the woman is infertile—Pope Paul instructed, in effect, that Catholics can positively intend *not* to have children and still be in accordance with the natural law.[4] While directed purely at the issue of family planning within marriage, Pope Paul's instruction also may have the effect of challenging the natural law defense of homosexuality outlined above. If procreative intent is no longer a determining factor in the morality of the sex act, then the fact that some homosexual couples possess it becomes irrelevant. Whether, though, Pope Paul's instruction on natural family planning is consistent with the teachings of Aquinas and other Catholics on sexuality—including Pope Pius's instruction on infertility within marriage—is highly doubtful. The resulting tension is the subject of considerable and continuing debate in Catholic and non-Catholic circles alike.

What the lively contemporary debate about the natural law and sexuality does show is that Aquinas's influence continues to be profound. Our modern notions about the rights and wrongs and, yes, the ins and outs of sex are tied inextricably to the simple idea that there is a law of nature that is shared by all, that is accessible by reason, and that should be obeyed.

These same, simple concepts about that law also shape much of our contemporary debate about violence, warfare, and even abortion. We'll see how in the next two chapters.

CHAPTER SEVEN

"Just War" and Double Effect

On January 28, 1991, President George Bush gave an address on American military involvement in Iraq (the so-called Gulf War). Two days earlier, the United States and its allies had initiated massive air bombing of Iraq. As CNN broadcast dramatic footage of Iraqi tracers and U.S. "smart" bombs igniting the night skies over Baghdad, President Bush offered his first public comments about the morality of the military action that just had been undertaken.

In his address, Bush claimed, "The war in the gulf is not a Christian war, a Jewish war, or a Muslim war—it is a just

war."[1] On what basis could he make such a proclamation? Bush cited several criteria for a just war. There must be, he said, a "just cause"—a legitimate moral reason to fight the war in the first place. Regarding the Gulf War, he asserted, "Our cause could not be more noble. We seek Iraq's withdrawal from Kuwait—completely, immediately, and without condition." Next, he said, the war must be declared by a "legitimate authority," and he went on to cite resolutions passed by both the U.S. Congress and the United Nations Security Council supporting the war. War must be a "last resort"—all peaceful means of righting the injustice must be exhausted before violence is initiated. Bush claimed that tireless diplomatic efforts to resolve the allies' differences with Iraq had failed. One also must have a "just intent," seeking justice rather than revenge. In each case, Bush indicated that the United States and its allies had met the criteria for a just war.

Just war? For the uninitiated, the very concept may seem like an oxymoron. To such individuals, Bush's speech, filled with moral rules and principles meant to restrain the execution of war, must seem strange indeed. After all, is not war what happens when moral codes break down? Isn't war the *absence* of morality?

Not according to international law. Even in times of war, modern international law demands that one follow moral guidelines—respect the rights of noncombatants, care for prisoners of war, and so forth. One is expected to fight wars only in response to legitimate causes, initiate war only as a last resort, and declare the war through proper channels. In short, one is expected to follow roughly the rules set forth by President Bush in his speech. Whether or not the United States actually followed these rules during the Gulf War is a more controversial matter and a question for another day. (One group of American Catholic bishops received much attention for claiming that the United States did not.) But the existence of some such rules—moral limits, in effect, on the fighting of war—is widely accepted. If there were no such limits—if war truly meant the absence of moral constraints—then why would so many people feel not merely horror but genuine moral outrage in the face of the abuses of the Nazis during World War II? If *anything* goes during war, then can the Nazis be judged to be any more immoral than anyone else?

For many of us, there *are* rules of war. Morality places important restraints on actions even during the heat of combat. The interesting question here, of course, is: From where did these rules come? Who says that this or that is the way that war morally must be fought? A simple but not entirely inaccurate answer is "Thomas Aquinas." (If you thought I was going to say "Gandhi," you obviously haven't been paying attention.)

Since the fourth century, when Christians went from being a persecuted minority to the ruling group in the Roman Empire, Christians have been rethinking their

views on war and violence. Before their ascent to political power, the vast majority of Christians assumed that one had to be a pacifist in order to be a Christian. After all, Jesus taught his followers to "turn the other cheek" and to "love your enemy." He died on the cross rather than use force to resist his persecutors. Surely his followers must adhere to his model and reject physical violence.

When Christians suddenly became the ruling group in the fourth century (it was during this time that Constantine became the first Christian ruler of the Roman

Empire), all this began to change. Led by the ideas of Augustine, Christians began to ask whether their "love of neighbor" could allow them to stand by while innocents were slaughtered. Shouldn't they intervene in defense of neighbor?[2]

Augustine was one of the first influential Christians to answer this question with a yes. Augustine taught that it was acceptable, even mandatory, for Christians to use violence—if they did so in a limited fashion and in order to protect the innocent. Augustine, in his *City of God,* is often credited with coining the term "just war" to describe precisely such undertakings.[3]

Eight centuries later, Aquinas, the great system-builder of Christianity, was crucial in developing and then codifying many of the concepts introduced by Augustine and other earlier Christians. When precisely can one go to war? What is an acceptable use of force in defense of neighbor? What is unacceptable?

Once again, we can turn to Aquinas's *Summa Theologica* (in this case, part II-II, q.40, a.1) for his answers. In it,

Aquinas offers one of the first detailed statements of the criteria that must be met before one rightfully can go to war. This will later become the so-called *jus ad bellum*. This is Latin for, roughly, "right or justice at (the time of) war," and if you're already familiar with the term, you need to start getting out more. In everyday language, the *jus ad bellum* consists of the conditions that must be met before one legitimately can go to war.

Aquinas argues that there are three such conditions, *each* of which must be satisfied before violence can be initiated. There must be a *just cause*: "A just war is . . . one that avenges wrongs, when a nation or state has to be punished for refusing to make amends for wrongs inflicted by its subjects, or to restore what it has seized unjustly." Next, the war must be declared by a *just authority*. Of the highest civil authority (kings and princes), Aquinas says, "Just as it is lawful for them to have recourse to the sword in defending the common weal against internal disturbances . . . so too it is their business to have recourse to the sword of war in defending the common weal against external enemies." Finally, even if the war is fought for a just cause and declared by a just authority, it is not a just war unless it is fought with a *just intent*. Aquinas lists as unacceptable such motivations as "the passion for inflicting harm, the cruel thirst for vengeance . . . the lust of power, and such like things." One must fight to restore justice, plain and simple, not to sate one's personal desires.[4]

These principles, of course, are almost verbatim the ones that President Bush appealed to in defending American actions in the Persian Gulf. Philosophers who followed Aquinas—especially the so-called scholastics such as Hugo Grotius and Francisco Suárez—subsequently would add to the list of *jus ad bellum* criteria. But Aquinas was the first thinker to codify and popularize many of the standards for when one rightfully may go to war. These standards are still in use today.

Aquinas's contributions to our modern ideas of war and violence do not end with his notions of when one may go to war. Aquinas also was pivotal in shaping our current views of what acts can and cannot be done once war begins. (These rules establishing moral standards for behavior once war has been initiated became known as the *jus in bello,* or "right/justice in war.")

This brings us to one of Aquinas's most important (and dreaded) contributions to our modern moral lexicon—the principle of *double effect.* Double effect is a moral concept that has found its way into our contemporary civil and criminal legal codes, has emerged as a cornerstone of medical ethics, and has become a sticking point in the modern

abortion debate. It also establishes the basic standard for determining how one must treat noncombatants in times of war. It thus deserves our careful attention. (Sure, you say "fine" now, but wait until I begin to explain some of the details. You'll be clamoring for some more discussion of fornication in no time.)

The starting premise for double effect is simple. As Aquinas notes, "Nothing hinders one act from having two effects," one good and the other bad.[5] In fact, most of the actions that occupy our attention in morality are of this sort. The reason is simple. If an action produces only good results (e.g., by giving Grandma some medicine, you make her feel better and, say, help whiten her teeth), there's no moral quandary. On the other hand, if an action produces only bad results (e.g., by giving Grandma the medicine, you kill her and you put other people at grave risk), there's likewise little moral debate. The cases that are morally interesting are those with a *double* effect, one good and one bad. For instance, what if the medicine you give Grandma will cure her while simultaneously posing a risk of spreading her ailment to others? Or what if the medicine eases her pain but has the side effect of hastening her death? In these types of cases, it's not immediately clear what the moral course of action should be. Is it right to help Grandma at a risk to others? Is it appropriate to make her more comfortable at a cost of shortening her life? Aquinas's notion of double effect attempts to give us a means of answering such tough moral questions.

One potential response—and one advocated by some Christians historically—is a simple one: Do no harm. If your action causes harm, pain, or risk to anyone, you should refrain from it. This may be, in part, the thinking of the Christian pacifists of the first four centuries. But Aquinas found this view impractical.

Take the following example. You have a severe toothache and go to see your dentist. She takes a look at your tooth, determines that you have a cavity, pulls out her drill, and pauses. You see, while she knows that drilling and filling the cavity is necessary to cure your toothache, she also knows that doing so will cause you great immediate pain. Plus, after the painkiller wears off, you will suffer considerably before the ultimate cure is effected. There will be a double effect caused by her drilling, one good (your toothache ultimately will be cured) and one bad (in the short term, much greater and more intense pain will be caused to you). If your dentist adhered to the simple standard, "Do no harm," she would walk away, never touching the drill to your tooth. Your tooth would continue to ache, but at least *she* would not be the cause of your pain. She would have done no harm.

Aquinas thought such a position was ridiculous. There are many cases that we face where some evil must be caused to achieve a greater good. To say we can never do any harm is to paralyze ourselves morally.

This is where the principle of double effect comes into play. What if, Aquinas asks, in an instance in which there is a double effect, only one of the effects is intended "while the other is beside the intention." According to Aquinas, "Moral acts take their species according to what is intended, and not according to what is beside the intention, since this is accidental."[6] This is the same concept we

saw employed in our discussion of the infertile couple and sex. If the couple's *intent* is to procreate, then whether or not a particular sex act results in conception is beside the point. The moral nature of the act is defined, at least in part, by the intention. We now can apply this same concept to the case of the dentist to see how Aquinas's logic has become commonplace in our thinking. What makes her drilling your tooth perfectly acceptable (to most of us) is the fact that her intent is to cure your toothache—not to inflict harm. She intends the good (curing you) and does not intend the evil (the pain that drilling causes). The latter is an accident in the metaphysical sense we discussed in chapter 4. It is not *essential* to her curing your toothache that you feel pain when she drills; if you are the lucky and rare individual immune to such pain, your toothache will still be cured by the drilling and filling. The pain is incidental to the cure.

Now let's introduce a change in our case of the dentist to see Aquinas's point about the importance of intent. Assume for the moment that you go to your dentist, but in this case your dentist is a sadist. She takes pleasure in inflicting pain. So she pulls out her drill and lets you have it, thoroughly enjoying her part in your agony. Even if she could minimize the pain, she would not seek to do so. Causing you pain, not curing you, is her point now. In this new scenario, our moral assessment of the dentist obviously would change dramatically. Rather than a kindly and competent dentist (as in the first scenario), she would be judged a psychopath. She would be subject to criminal charges. Aquinas would say that this change in our opinion of the dentist is entirely appropriate and is due to the dramatic shift in the dentist's *intent* between the two cases. Before, the dentist intended you to be cured and the pain was accidental. Now she intends to inflict pain. Aquinas does not think that the crucial issue is necessarily the difference between the *results* of her actions in the two scenarios, that is, the fact that in one case you are cured of the toothache and in the other case not. Assume for a moment that, by pure accident, the sadistic dentist—intent on causing you pain—should by chance happen upon a decaying tooth and drill it. The result is that she cures your toothache, though this was not her aim at all. The result in this case may be a good one, but Aquinas thinks we should still judge the dentist harshly. She still acted immorally, even though the results of her actions may have turned out to be beneficial.

If you follow the above argument, then you have grasped one-half of the principle of double effect. What Aquinas tells us is that if a single act has two effects, one good and one bad, the act is only possibly permissible if you intend the good end and do not intend the evil end.

This concept may seem arcane and abstract, but it is at the heart of many of our modern moral notions. For instance, something very much like Aquinas's concept of intent is crucial to the legal concept of murder. If, while backing out of your driveway, you run over and kill your neighbor's toddler, it makes a world of legal difference whether the act was accidental or intentional. If it can be shown to be an accident—you had no animosity for the child, you exercised every caution in backing up, the toddler suddenly crawled from behind the bushes after you had checked to see if the driveway was clear—you in all likelihood will not be charged with any crime. If, on the other hand, it can be shown that your intent was to kill the child—you had made threats to the child's life before, you saw him in the driveway before you put the car in reverse, upon backing up and missing the child you put the car in forward and set aim again—you will be convicted of murder. The difference between the two cases, Aquinas would point out, is not the result. In each case the child is dead. The difference? Intent.

Aquinas's concept of intent also has become a cornerstone of the *jus in bello*—the rules for determining which acts are permissible in times of war (though Aquinas himself never explicitly applied it to wartime situations). One application of the concept to warfare is the idea that soldiers must never intend the death of innocents or noncombatants. This is most pointedly *not* to say that innocents will never be killed (any more than the good dentist can promise that pain will never be inflicted). It is rather to say that the death of innocents, when it occurs, must be accidental (i.e., unintended). The point must be to

aim at legitimate military targets, not innocents. Once again we see here the importance of Aquinas's metaphysics. Just as a triangle has certain characteristics accidental to its being a triangle (e.g., its size, its color), so too, according to Aquinas, our actions may have characteristics accidental to their essences. Of course, defining which characteristics of a human act are accidental and which are essential becomes quite complicated.

An example or two might help illustrate how Aquinas tries to draw this tricky line. Say that your military seeks to bomb an enemy munitions factory. This factory will soon be producing chemical weapons of great risk to your side and

so bombing it would be a "good" (save lives in the future, help you defeat an unjust opponent, and so forth). Unfortunately, the munitions factory is directly adjacent to a twenty-four-hour day care center. At all times of the day, children (i.e., innocents) are sleeping and playing just a few yards away from the factory. What Aquinas's principle suggests is that the act of bombing the factory may be permissible even if you believe that it will kill some of the innocent children. How? If your intent is to knock out the factory and not to kill children, then the death of those children becomes accidental—not part of the essence of your act. And how do we know that the death of the children is not part of that essence (i.e., not intended)? The death of the children is neither your end nor the means to your end, Aquinas tells us. If you drop the bomb and flatten the factory, and, by some miracle, the rubble falls and not a single child is killed, your good end is still achieved. You have knocked out the chemical weapons factory. The death of the children (like the pain you feel when a dentist drills your cavity) is not essential to the good end that is intended.

Now imagine a case in which your side is all but defeated by a dangerous foe. Desperate to turn the tide in the war and down to your last few fighter planes, you decide to "demoralize" your opponent. The children of the enemy's leadership are in the aforementioned day care center. If you bomb the center and kill the children, the enemy's leadership—who are fighting the war for the benefit of future generations of their nation—may give up the war effort. You give the go ahead and bomb the day care center. The results may be the same as in the case of targeting the adjacent chemical weapons plant: The children in the day care center are killed. But Aquinas would judge the two cases entirely differently. In the second scenario, your *intent* is to kill the innocent. The death of the children is essential to your achieving the goal of demoralizing your opponent; it is the means to your end. In this case, if you drop the bombs and, by some miracle, no children are killed, you must reload and bomb again. For Aquinas, it is the second case, but not necessarily the first, that must be condemned as immoral.

During the Gulf War, there was a famous incident in which U.S. bombers hit what turned out to be a civilian air-raid shelter in Baghdad. Many women, children, and other noncombatants were killed. Iraqi officials immediately gave the world press access to the site, and pictures of the carnage soon filled the airwaves. Within hours, U.S. generals Colin Powell and H. Norman Schwarzkopf were holding a news conference to defend the action. Their defense? The principle of double effect. Powell and Schwarzkopf did not deny that innocents had been killed by the bombing. What they claimed is that the death of civilians had not been the *intent*. The best information they had, they asserted, had indicated that the building in question was an Iraqi military command post. The intent had been to knock out the military command, not to kill women and children. This was a case in which there was a double effect, they claimed, and the United States intended the good end.

For anyone acquainted with Aquinas, the argument of the U.S. military leaders was a familiar one. In fact, Aquinas's principle of double effect has become so integral to the waging of modern war that it has even acquired in recent years a euphemistic new label: "collateral damage." When one seeks to strike legitimate military targets and accidentally (i.e., unintentionally) ends up killing civilians, military leaders often (and, some people think, irritatingly) refer to such deaths with the sanitized term "collateral damage." Thank (or blame) Aquinas for this.

We are not quite through with double effect yet. (I warned you that the principle was a complicated one.) You see, even if you have a good intent—even if you can show that you intend the good and not the evil—in a case of double effect, there is a second consideration. Does the good effect outweigh the evil one? As Aquinas writes, "And yet, though proceeding from a good intention, an act may be rendered unlawful, if it be out of proportion to the end."[7] In short, your act must result in more good than evil. Let's go back to our example of the munitions factory. Even if our intent is to knock out the factory and not to kill nearby children, Aquinas tells us that our act is still morally wrong if its good effects are not proportionate to its evil ones. Let's say that the factory, if bombed, will be out of service for only a few hours. By mid-afternoon, it will be up and producing chemical weapons again. Let's also say that not a handful but hundreds of children will be killed in the bombing of the plant. In such a situation, Aquinas would say that the bombing is wrong—not because our intent is bad but because the evil created is disproportionate to the good. Our act will produce more evil than good.

Thus, when employing the principle of double effect, there are two questions to ask: "Do you intend the good (and not the evil) end?" and "Does the good end outweigh the evil one?" Only if the answer to *both* questions is yes can you say, according to Aquinas, that the action is morally justified.

Again, these may seem to be wildly abstract and technical philosophical principles. But Aquinas's influence has been so sizable that they have become an integral part of our common moral debates—in courts, on the battlefield, even when backing out of driveways.

One of the most interesting (and surprising) ways that double effect is applied to contemporary issues is seen in the example of abortion. In the next chapter, we'll take a brief look at the implications of Aquinas's arguments for the modern debate about abortion. We'll also see how Aquinas's views on natural law pose challenges to modern understandings of the roles and rights of women.

CHAPTER EIGHT

Abortion, the Role of Women,
and Other Noncontroversial Issues

Almost everyone knows that Catholicism historically has condemned abortion with great fervency. With our discussion of the principle of double effect, we now can see part of the reason why. If one assumes that the fetus is a full person (admittedly, a debatable moral assumption), abortion becomes condemnable to the follower of Aquinas because it fails both of the two tests of double effect: the evil end (the death of an innocent person) is intended and the good end (the mother's desire not to bear the child) does not outweigh it. This has been the mainstream Catholic argument on abortion for decades.

What is surprising (perhaps even to some Catholics) is that, if I have interpreted double effect properly, there is at least one case in which abortion becomes permissible, even by the standards of Aquinas. Many people believe that once one assumes that the fetus is a full moral person, then all acts of abortion become murder (i.e., the intentional killing of the innocent). The supporter of Aquinas's concept of double effect would not necessarily agree.

Take the case of a pregnancy that threatens the life of the mother. In cases of ectopic pregnancy, for instance, the fertilized egg implants in the mother's fallopian tube rather

than in her uterus. If not removed, the developing zygote (i.e., the fertilized egg in its early development) will cause the fallopian tube to rupture and potentially will kill the mother. Is removing the zygote morally permissible, even if we say that such life is a full person?

If I have interpreted Aquinas's principle of double effect correctly, he would say, "Yes, abort the zygote" (or, more precisely, "Yes, remove the diseased tissue"). How so? Well, here we have a classic case of double effect. By removing the developing zygote, we create a good end (we save the mother's life) and a bad one (we kill a "person," the zygote). But Aquinas would ask that we pose those two, by-now-familiar questions.

First, is the good end our intent and the evil one unintended? In this case, the answers are yes and yes. We seek to save the mother's life. The death of the zygote is not our intent. How do we know this? Here again we turn to some of the terminology that Aquinas introduces in his discussion of metaphysics. The death of the zygote is not *essential* to our good end—it is not the means to our end. The zygote's removal—not death—is what is sought. If by some miracle the zygote—only a few days old—should live once it is removed from the mother, the good end still would be achieved. The mother's life still would be saved. The death of the zygote is not the means to our saving the mother's life. It is *accidental*, in Aquinas's terminology. (This contrasts, for instance, with our earlier example of trying to demoralize the enemy by bombing the day care center. There, the death of the innocents was essential to achieving the good end of disheartening the enemy and winning the war.)

Second, does the act produce more good than evil? Again, the answer seems to be yes. If we do nothing, both the mother and the zygote will die (the mother from the

rupture of her fallopian tube, the zygote because it will not reach viability before the mother expires). If we remove the zygote, we at least save one life, namely, the mother's. The act is proportionate by Aquinas's standard. Thus, neither aspect of double effect is violated by our aborting the fetus in this case.

This is a surprising conclusion in many ways. One thing that many people think they know about Catholicism is that it always opposes abortion. But if one applies the arguments of Aquinas, the most orthodox of all Catholic thinkers, to cases of abortion involving a threat to the mother's life, one discovers a case in which abortion may well be judged permissible. Of course, whether or not the above scenario represents a case of abortion at all depends in large part on how one defines abortion. If abortion is defined as the intentional killing of a fetus, then our case of ending an ectopic pregnancy does not constitute an abortion at all, since the death of the fetus is unintended (i.e., incidental and accidental to the end of saving the mother's life). On the other hand, if abortion is defined as the premature removal of a fetal life resulting in its death, then the ectopic scenario does indeed constitute an abortion—and an abortion of which Aquinas would approve.

We now have seen ways in which Thomas Aquinas's concept of natural law has shaped our modern notions on such issues as sex, war, and abortion (and even dentistry). In many ways, my argument has been that Aquinas's views are very much in tune with modern, mainstream beliefs on these topics. Aquinas was a thinker ahead of his time, and he paved the way for many of today's most significant legal and moral concepts.

There is at least one area, however, where this is not the case—where Aquinas's views are increasingly out of sync with contemporary beliefs. In exploring this area, we will confront one important drawback to the natural law approach that Aquinas was so instrumental in popularizing.

The subject in question is the role of women. In his arguments on this topic, Aquinas was not all that atypical of medieval men in general. According to Aquinas, woman is, by her very nature, a helper to man. In fact, he argues that her helpfulness is specifically and (almost) exclusively in the area of procreation. Listen to his words from the *Summa Theologica*: "It was necessary for woman to be made as a helper to man; not, indeed, helpmate in other works, as some say, since man can be more efficiently helped by another man in other works; but as a helper in generation."[1] Women, he says in effect, are needed by men, but they are needed for the purpose of producing off-spring. If man desires an intellectual companion, a conversation partner, or someone to help him build a house, he is much better served by selecting a male "helpmate" than a female "helper." Indeed, women are by nature ill-equipped to serve such functions.

In Aquinas's estimation, God has naturally endowed woman with certain intellectual and rational faculties, but just as the intellect of humanity is a poor approximation of that of the angels, so woman's intellectual faculties are but a cloudy reflection of man's. While both male and female are necessary for reproduction, "man is yet further ordered to a still nobler vital action, and that is intellectual operation."[2]

This discrepancy in intellectual abilities leads to a natural hierarchy between male and female in which the male always should predominate: "For good order would have been wanting if some were not governed by others wiser than themselves. So by such a kind of subjection woman is naturally subject to man, because in man the discretion of reason predominates."[3] This gender inequality, Aquinas assures us, was the cause of—not caused by—Eve's yielding to temptation in the garden of Eden. In other words, it was not as punishment for Eve's sin that women are less reasonable than and subject to men; it is the fact that women are these things by their very nature which explains why Eve was the first to sin. This may seem a fine distinction, but it is an important one. If the inequality between male and female precedes the fall, as Aquinas here claims, then it is part of God's intended, natural order. To use the by-now-familiar terms, it is not an accident but part of the created essence of women that they be subject to men—and the sin in the garden of Eden becomes not only one of

humanity's disobedience to God but one of woman usurping the authority of man.

This judgment that women are inferior to men extends to Aquinas's portrayal of the procreation of the species. Women, Aquinas suggests, are merely the vessel in which new life is incubated. To use modern, scientific terminology, they are not genetic contributors to the new human life. Aquinas draws an analogy here to planting a seed in the ground. Man provides and plants the seed that will generate into a human; woman simply provides the medium for the seed's germination.

Like the other arguments of Aquinas that we have discussed, his views about women would become hugely influential. Of course, his ideas were, in one sense, not novel at all: The powers that be—almost exclusively male—thought women to be inferior long before Aquinas came along. In another sense, however, his views added a new dimension to sexism. Instead of "merely" being a claim of priests and scriptures, the superiority of men to women was now a "rational" fact, a cornerstone of the natural law and science, and thus a truism for all peoples in all places. When priests and scriptures were called into question with the rise of secularism, the natural law arguments against women remained.

And this should provide a warning to all of us about our use of natural law, whether we are discussing sexuality, war, abortion, or women. One great challenge posed by the natural law, although often overlooked by its advocates, is the need to distinguish between *what is* and *what should be*. As we have seen, Aquinas lived an insulated life. At the age of five, he was sent off to a Benedictine monastery—an all-male environment. He later attended the all-male University of Naples and joined the all-male Dominican order before going on to teach at the all-male University of Paris. He never married and probably never engaged in sex with a woman. He had precious few experiences with women whatsoever. He lived in a world in which women were subject to men, were not seen as intellectual entities but as carnal ones, and were dominated by men socially, politically, and legally. Given this set of experiences, we can hardly find it surprising (though some of us still find it disappointing) that Aquinas looked out into the world and declared that women were "naturally" subject to men. That's what he saw around him. It must be, he thought, the way God had intended the natural order to be.

But using the natural law demands that we do more than report on the way things are. Murders and thefts occur every day—and science now believes that humans have a genetic proclivity toward aggression—but Aquinas does not want to say that these acts are natural and approved of by God. Studies show that the majority of Americans cheat on their income taxes, but Aquinas would not want to declare cheating on taxes natural and thus a dictate of the natural law. What *is* is not always what *should be*. Similarly, the fact that women were not the intellectual equals of men in A.D. 1250—a time in which women were excluded summarily from almost all educational and intellectual pursuits—does not necessarily mean that the situation was God-intended. Aquinas should have known better.

But the fact of the matter is that it is notoriously difficult to distinguish between *what is* and *what is natural*. When slavery was being contested in the Americas, many opponents of change made a version of the following natural law argument: "Blacks are, in the American South of the 1800s, uneducated and enslaved. Therefore, the subjugation of blacks must be part of God's natural, created plan. To abolish slavery is to violate the natural law." Most of us now see the error—and the horrible injustice—of this argument.

But Aquinas's discussion of women shows how easy it is for even the brightest of us to fall prey to a like error, how easy it is to assume that what is familiar to us is what is natural and hence God-intended. At one point in his discussion of politics (see chapter 9), Aquinas advocates the rule of one monarch over his kingdom. To justify his stance, Aquinas writes that "in the hive, the bees have one king."[4]

It is a silly remark, made in passing, but it's telling. To someone living in medieval times, it was only natural to assume that the head of the hive must be the "king bee." Rulers who dominate and lead are male; females are subservient and meek. If this is true of human society, it *must* be true of the animal kingdom as well. It was a plausible assumption. But it was wrong.

Aquinas's historically influential natural law approach to moral issues offers an incredible opportunity for its advocates to overcome the shackles of tradition. In the hands of Thomas Jefferson or Martin Luther King Jr., as we'll see in the next chapter, Aquinas's theories can be the source of liberating justice. They allow one to say, "Sure, things have always been done this way, but nature (and God) demand that we do otherwise." Aquinas himself often applied his natural law theories in just this manner, at times making great strides in issues of human justice. (We'll discuss a few such instances in the upcoming chapter.) But lurking just beneath the surface of any use of the natural law is a risk:

Rather than catching a glimpse of the ways of God and nature, we may be holding a mirror up to ourselves. We may be confusing what is natural for what is familiar and comfortable. And there is often a world of difference between what is familiar and comfortable and what is just.

Let's take a closer look at exactly what is just according to Aquinas, and how this serves to shape his views on politics and the civil law.

CHAPTER NINE

Politics

"How does one determine when a law is just or unjust? A just law is a man-made code that squares with the moral law or the law of God. An unjust law is a code that is out of harmony with the moral law. To put it in the terms of Saint Thomas Aquinas, an unjust law is a law that is not rooted in eternal and natural law. Any law that uplifts human personality is just. Any law that degrades human personality is unjust."

These words extolling Aquinas's approach to the law come not from a pope or a priest—not from a Catholic at

all—but from a Baptist minister. They were written on Easter weekend 1963 by Martin Luther King Jr. from his jail cell in Birmingham, Alabama.[1] Three days earlier, King had been arrested for protesting the segregationist laws in that city and for holding a public demonstration without a permit. In a public letter to the clergy of Birmingham—many of whom had condemned him as a lawbreaker and rabble-rouser—King attempted to justify his actions. His appeal, significantly, was to Thomas Aquinas.

Can it ever be right to disobey the laws of the state? Is breaking the law permissible if the laws themselves are unjust? Until Aquinas came onto the scene, the answer for most Christians to both questions was an unqualified no. Based in part upon a controversial reading of Paul (especially his views in Romans 13) and a superficial reading of Augustine (especially his *City of God*), many Christians held that disobeying a king or a prince was the equivalent of disobeying God. After all, the all-powerful God rules creation down to the tiniest hair on your head. Surely he appoints those who rule and determines which laws they enact. As Augustine writes, "Thus it happens, but not without God's providence, that some are endowed with kingdoms and others made subject to kings."[2] To disobey the state is to disobey God.

If this view of politics were true, then the likes of Thomas Jefferson and Martin Luther King Jr. would be lost. Jefferson could not protest the taxation practices of England's king—for God, in his infinite wisdom, has determined that King George rule. And Martin Luther King Jr., a black man, could not sit down at a "white only" lunch counter in Birmingham; if Birmingham was led by segregationists and governed by racist laws, then this too must be God's will. Revolution and its milder cousin, civil disobedience, both would become morally unacceptable by definition. Even the worst tyrant would be seen as God-appointed—and would have to be obeyed by the Christian steadfastly.

In his work *On Princely Government* (also known as *On Kingship*), Aquinas presents a very different view.[3] Just as each human person has an ultimate end, Aquinas tell us, so too does every king, every prince, and every principality. And the end for each is precisely the same: the good, which is God. The king and the state only fulfill their God-established essence when they pursue the good; when they pursue evil ends, they have not only defaulted

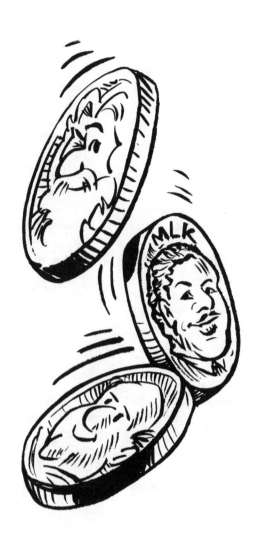

on their assigned responsibilities but they also (at least in one sense) are no longer "the king" and "the state" at all (since kings and states *by definition,* for Aquinas, pursue justice and the good).

Based upon this simple premise and borrowing heavily from Aristotle, Aquinas offers what has become a famous classification of six different types of government, ranking them according to desirability. In many ways, Aquinas's ranking here is reminiscent of his ranking of sexual sins discussed in chapter 6. We have a desired end—in this case, the common good, which is God—and, as in Aquinas's discussion of sex, different acts become more or less just depending on how closely they achieve that end. The further from the established end that it deviates, the more unjust an act becomes.

By this logic, *monarchy* is the most desirable form of government, Aquinas tells us. Monarchy is rule by a single leader, a king, who in his actions pursues the just end of the common good, or God. (Given our discussion of women in the last chapter, it is perhaps not surprising that Aquinas does not consider the possibility of a female monarch.) What makes monarchy the best form of government? It is both good in intent and efficient in practice. It is good because the monarch is dedicated to the just end, which is God. It is efficient because, as a single ruler, he is like the captain of a ship, guiding the vessel that is the state to its appointed port without dissent and contention. His good rule is unchallenged, and his focus is keen.

The next most desirable form of government is what Aquinas calls *aristocracy.* Aristocracy in Aquinas's nomenclature is rule by a few individuals who all are seeking the common good—God. Imagine a U.S. Senate in which each senator was utterly dedicated to justice and pursued the common good exclusively rather than acting for

political or personal gain. (Admittedly, you may have to stretch your imagination just a bit here.) Such a government would be very good, Aquinas thinks, though not quite as desirable as a monarchy. What is the shortcoming of aristocracy? Efficiency. While the senators' intent is the good, they inevitably will have different visions of it. While one senator might seek to help the elderly, another might work to improve education. Yet they still must vote as a unit and decide which of the various proposals are to be implemented. As a result, not as much gets done. (You don't have to stretch your imagination to envision a Senate like *that*.)

Next most desirable is *polity*. This is rule by the many (or "everyone," though Aquinas never envisioned women to be included among "everyone"), each of whom is pursuing the common good or God. It's a good form of government, since everyone's heart is in the right place, but, Aquinas tells us, it is wildly inefficient. Even well-meaning individuals have such divergent notions of what the good demands that important matters get bogged down in endless debate and compromise. Such is the drawback of polity.

Next come the unjust forms of government. All of these are defined as unjust by the fact that the individual(s) involved seek(s) self-gain rather than the common good. The least unjust of the unjust forms of government, according to Aquinas, is *democracy*. Many modern readers will find it surprising, even shocking, that Aquinas classified democracy as an *unjust* form of government, but we

pursue the common good; it is more unjust than democracy because it is more efficient in attaining unjust ends.

The most efficient—and hence most unjust—form of unjust government, Aquinas tells us, is *tyranny*. Like monarchy, this is rule by a single individual, but tyranny is characterized by a leader who seeks his own selfish ends. Without any competing power—without any checks and balances—the tyrant is able to lead his people to great injustices. Think of Adolf Hitler. It's not just the fact that Hitler had evil ends that made his rule so damaging; unfortunately, there are lots of politicians like that. His significance rests in the fact that he was so evil *and* so effective in leading people to his evil ends. With no one in Germany able or willing to challenge his political power, he brought his vision of a "final solution" horrifyingly close to completion. It is just this efficiency that makes tyranny the least desirable form of government.

The astute follower of Aquinas will note a dilemma here. If you are concerned with establishing a new government, it seems that Aquinas is saying that you both should and should not opt for rule by a single individual. If the leader turns out to be just, you have established a monarchy—the most desirable form of government. But if the ruler turns out to be unjust, you are left with a tyranny—the very worst form of government. What should you do?

At least in *On Princely Government,* Aquinas says to chance it, to adopt a government in which one person holds all the power. Why should we pursue such a risky path? Here is another place where Aquinas's optimism about humanity is evidenced. Just as he thinks humans, in general, are smart enough to learn truths about God through their reason and intellect (see chapter 2) and moral enough to engage in sex without being overcome by pleasure (see chapter 6), so too Aquinas thinks humans, in general, are good enough to rule justly. Yes, he reasons, rule by a single individual is problematic, but only if that individual is unjust. And *people tend to be just.* Besides, he tells us, good tends to be stronger than evil—since there is but one ultimate good (God) yet as many evils as there are individual goals and ends. Good and its supporters are unified; evil tends to divide. Thus, far more often than not, good wins out over evil. Hence, it makes sense to support a government in which one person holds all of the power, even though such a government *could* become tyrannical.

Years later, in the *Summa Theologica*, Aquinas qualified this view.[4] Perhaps a lifetime's worth of experience helped to temper the optimism of his youth, but Aquinas came to advocate a mixed form of government in which a monarch's rule would be checked by an aristocracy (a powerful but small group of elected leaders), and both of these, in turn, would be checked by a polity (all of the governed who would come together to elect the aristocrats). It is in reading Aquinas's views on government in the *Summa* that

one is most struck by the parallels between his arguments and the philosophy behind the founding of the American governmental system. Like Madison would do centuries later, Aquinas holds that people are generally good; their wisdom and experience is to be tapped. But one must do so with caution and with "checks and balances" set up to prevent perverse results. In fact, as Madison would do five hundred years later, Aquinas in the *Summa* sets up a "tripartite" system (i.e., a government with three separate bodies) to serve as a safeguard against the excesses of any one branch: "Such is the best government, formed by a good mixture of kingship, in the sense that one person is the chief, and aristocracy, in the sense that many men rule according to virtue, and polity (that is, the power of the people), in the sense that leaders can be elected from among the populace, and further, the choice of the rule belongs to the people."[5]

In such passages, one also can begin to see why Aquinas was so popular with the likes of Thomas Jefferson and Martin Luther King Jr. Aquinas's vision of government is not the so-called divine rights of kings—the view in which kings are appointed by God and their edicts bear the same force as an edict from God himself. No, Aquinas sets up a subtler system. Even a true monarch—the king whose power is unchecked by aristocrats and the polity—gains his right to rule from the people and is worthy of obedience only when he pursues the common good, which is God. Doing so is essential to his being a king in the first place. A ruler who pursues unjust ends is not, by Aquinas's definition, a king at all. He is a tyrant. And no tyrant is owed our allegiance. The same is true with rule by the few (aristocracy/oligarchy) and rule by everyone (polity/democracy). In each case, when these governments pursue the good, they must be obeyed. When they swerve from the path of justice, they become unjust institutions. Your moral obligation remains to the common good, not to outlaws. (Aquinas does suggest that, while not owed our allegiance, unjust forms of government at times should receive it—if only for practical reasons. The price of rebellion is often more costly than bearing up under tyranny, he cautions.)

Moreover, and this is a point crucial to understanding his political philosophy, Aquinas points out that any just government will be obeyed *naturally* by any just individual. If your government, for instance, has a rule outlawing murder (a just rule) and you are a moral individual (following your reason to conform to the natural law), you have nothing to fear from the state. Indeed, the law does not constrain you in any way. Why? Because you have no inclination to murder. When you, as an individual citizen, are pursuing the common good via your reason and your lawmakers and leaders are pursuing the common good via their reason, there can be no conflict. You may live in a state with police, laws, and jails, but they don't constrain your inclinations. Only the unjust are shackled by a law against murder (or by any just law). And only *unjust* laws shackle the just.

This was a point not lost on Martin Luther King Jr. At one point in his "Letter from a Birmingham Jail," King, quoting Augustine, proclaimed that "an unjust law is no law at all." Like many ideas in the letter, this is a very Thomistic point. An unjust law is not worthy of obedience according to Aquinas because it is not a law at all. A law by definition is "an ordinance of reason directed to the common good."[6] To use the terminology from our discussion of metaphysics in chapter 4, it is an *essential attribute* of a law that it serve the good. Just as a geometric figure must have three sides in order to be a triangle, a civil rule must pursue the common good in order to be a law. If a government edict demanded, for example, that we torture babies, we would not be breaking the law by disobeying it—at least not by Aquinas's terminology. The edict would not, by definition, be a law at all; it would be a perversion of the law. Our obligation would remain to the common good, and our *disobedience* to the dictate would be morally mandatory.

This is an exceptional claim. At a time when much of Christendom doubted the ability of any individual to determine for himself or herself the worthiness of kings, princes, and laws, Aquinas set up a political system that had its basis in "the power of the people" and that demanded that citizens use their God-given attributes—their reason and intellect—to continually make judgments about right and wrong. This is a simple idea, but its effects would be revolutionary. As Aquinas writes, "Nor should the community be accused of disloyalty for deposing a tyrant, even after a previous promise of constant fealty [i.e., loyalty]; for

the tyrant lays himself open to such treatment by his failure to discharge the duties of his office as governor of the community, and in consequence his subjects are no longer bound by their oath to him."[7]

Was not Jefferson making just this point when he wrote in the Declaration of Independence, "Whenever any form of government becomes destructive of [its] ends, it is the right of the people to alter or to abolish it, and to institute a new government"? Was not King making just this point when he disobeyed the segregationist laws of a racist Birmingham, pointing out, "We can never forget that everything Hitler did in Germany was 'legal' and everything . . . the freedom fighters did . . . was 'illegal'"?[8] For Jefferson and King alike, the lawless are not those who oppose unjust edicts but those who issue them.

For Aquinas, as centuries later for Jefferson and for King, the "law" is by definition that which is just. An unjust law is no law at all. The concept is a simple one; the implications are, quite literally, revolutionary.

CHAPTER TEN

Reading Aquinas

Perhaps the last sentence of the previous chapter could serve as a slogan for the thought of Thomas Aquinas in general: The concepts are simple, but the impact has been revolutionary. (All right, I admit that the double effect stuff in chapter 7 was not all that simple.) I suspect modern society has tended to underestimate and underappreciate the contributions Aquinas has made to our thinking precisely because his views have become so mainstream, so common. We now are a society that exalts reason, that questions authority, that acknowledges human rights, that posits a natural law, that weighs intentionality in our criminal codes, that talks about just war, and, yes, that looks at the double effect of moral actions. If you are Roman Catholic, you, in addition, likely have conceptions of God, humans and angels, free will, birth control, premarital sex, abortion, and maybe even dentistry that have their roots in the arguments of an unassuming, thirteenth-century bookworm from Aquino, Italy.

Few philosophers have ever covered such a breadth of material in such detail. Few writers have challenged the reader more. Few thinkers have been so misunderstood. Thus, while I close this volume with the hope that you now are inspired enough to go out and explore Aquinas further and while I urge you to read some of his works for yourself, I must admit that the task is a daunting one.

Aquinas is difficult and quirky to read. His works tend to be long. (All right, they tend to be *really* long.) Somewhere amid Aquinas's fifteenth objection to an obscure point of theology, the average reader might well want to scream, "Get to the point!" (If you listen carefully the next time you drive by your local Catholic seminary, you just may hear these words wafting across the campus at night.)

Yet there are a few tricks that can make reading and understanding Aquinas a little easier.

Although Aquinas's life was brief—under fifty years—he left behind over sixty written works. For most scholars, reading Aquinas means tackling his mammoth work, the *Summa Theologica*. Most of the points about Aquinas that were covered in this book can be found in this incredible summation of theology. In the *Summa* (as it is commonly called), Aquinas rather modestly set out to create a simple manual of Christian doctrine for the use of students. He notes in the prologue that many theology books relied on at the time, disorganized and disjointed, "beget disgust

and confusion in the minds of learners." What Aquinas proposed to do, "confiding in Divine assistance," was to treat issues pertaining to sacred doctrine with "brevity and clearness." The result: thirty-eight treatises, subdivided into 3,120 articles, with about 10,000 objections posed and then answered. So much for brevity.

But the clearness *is* there, if you know how to read the text. The entire *Summa* is written in a question and answer format, with Aquinas both posing the questions and supplying the answers. In fact, each of the work's articles considers a particular question—ranging from the (somewhat) accessible like "Whether the highest good, God, is the cause of evil?" to the incredibly esoteric like "Whether the intelligible species abstracted from phantasms are related to our intellect as that which is understood?" (I kid you not.) In each case, Aquinas starts with a series of "objections" to the answer he eventually will adopt to the question. If he thinks God is not the source of evil, for instance, he first will summarize the arguments of authors who think (or who appear to think) that God *is* the source of evil. Don't make the silly mistake of taking the ideas expressed in the "objections" section as Aquinas's own beliefs. (Many freshmen theology papers have died quick and embarrassing deaths for just this mistake.) These "objections" represent, in most cases, the *opposite* of Thomas's own positions. He merely is recounting what others have said.

For each question, he next includes a (usually brief) section labeled "On the contrary" in which he cites authors who have taken up the opposite position on the same question.

Then comes a section beginning "I answer that . . ." Here's the place to look for Aquinas's own views on the question at hand. This is his own philosophy and theology articulated.

Finally, each question closes with "replies to objections," a section in which each of the objections cited at the outset of the question is responded to, one by one, with Aquinas usually explaining where the author in question goes wrong or how the author has been misread. This section, like the "I answer that . . ." section, represents Aquinas's own beliefs and arguments.

This same, strange format is followed faithfully 3,120 times in the *Summa*. So for each question that Aquinas poses, you will find the following sequence:

QUESTION	*On the contrary* . . .	* I ANSWER THAT . . .
Objection 1		* Reply to Objection 1
Objection 2		* Reply to Objection 2
Objection 3		* Reply to Objection 3
Objection 4		* Reply to Objection 4

*Note: * indicates Aquinas's own arguments and beliefs*

An example of how this all fleshes out in the pages of the *Summa Theologica* when words are added looks something like the following:

Question 7: Proteins
(in Thirty-Seven Articles)
First Article
Whether chunky or smooth be the more perfect form of peanut butter?

We proceed to the first article;

Objection 1: It would seem that chunky is the more perfect form of peanut butter. For Plato argues that a thing is more perfect as it more closely approaches its original form. But peanut butter takes the peanut as its original form; therefore chunky, having more of the perfection of the peanut, is the more perfect form of peanut butter.

Objection 2: Further, according to the Philosopher, that object is more perfect which contributes most directly to being, and that object is less perfect which detracts from being. Now, smooth detracts from being by means of its tendency to stick to the roof of the mouth, bonding the upper and lower palates. (There was that spate of tragic choking deaths in Sicily last year.) Therefore chunky is the more perfect form of peanut butter.

On the contrary, Peter and Paul together have declared, "Sometimes you feel like a nut; sometimes you don't."

I answer that, a thing may be perfect in two ways. The first is with regard to its means and the second with regard to its end. Now, smooth is the more perfect peanut butter with regard to the means since, due to its physical properties, it can serve as the means for not only nourishment but for bonding one's dentures, repairing tableware and, as Augustine points out, "performing acts so shameful and perverse that the multitudes of Carthage would pay to observe them." But chunky is the more perfect with regard to the end, as when Marcia Brady declares to her beloved housekeeper Alice, "Oh Alice, this sandwich is the living *end*." Hence, the wisdom of the angelic Saints Peter and Paul is confirmed: "Sometimes you feel like a nut; sometimes you don't."

Reply Obj. 1: Are you going to listen to Plato? The guy wore a dress.

Reply Obj. 2: An object may be less perfect in and of itself (I always forget the Latin for that), or it may be less perfect because of the way an object is employed. Hence a chalice, which is inherently a good object, becomes imperfect when it is embedded in the forehead of your Dominican brother who mocks you incessantly for being the "Dumb Ox." Similarly, smooth peanut butter, when not joined properly with the appropriate amount of jelly, causes the bonding of the upper and lower palates, as was the case in Sicily. Yet this speaks to the imperfection of the application of the peanut butter; not an imperfection of its being. Peanut butters do not kill; people do.

Now in case you haven't already guessed, these are not Aquinas's actual words. The culinary sections of the *Summa*, quite tragically, were never completed. (All right, he had no intention of adding a culinary section to the *Summa*—though given Aquinas's notorious love of food

149

and a few more years, who knows?) But the above example illustrates Aquinas's basic methodology: the posing of a question, the consideration of the opinions of other philosophers and theologians, and the offering of a rational synthesis of the various insights. In point of fact, for some questions he raises in the *Summa,* Aquinas offers not two "objections" and two "replies to objections" (as in the above example) but two *dozen* of each. Reading Aquinas can get very complex. If you want the condensed version of Aquinas's views, try reading the question at the outset of each article and then skipping directly to the section that Aquinas labels "I answer that . . . ." You'll get the gist of his argument without having to wade through a series of sometimes confusing objections to his position.

To truly appreciate the genius of Aquinas, however, take the time to read some sections of the *Summa* in their entirety. Pay attention to the amazing array of figures and texts cited and quoted by Aquinas—the Bible, the Greek philosopher Aristotle, the Jewish thinker Maimonides, the Muslim Avicenna, the Christian Augustine, and hundreds of others. Then remember that Aquinas wrote in a time before not only computers but modern libraries and reference texts. The ability to quote directly from such a range of thinkers, to immediately understand the implications of their arguments, and to draw connections between their ideas came from a very special mind—a mind that some consider unequaled in the history of Western thought.

If you are persistent, you will be rewarded. You will be exposed to Aquinas's views on an array of issues we have not been able even to touch upon in this volume: theological issues such as the nature of the incarnation and the significance of baptism; moral issues such as the centrality of the virtues and the problem with lying; psychological issues such as what constitutes a habit and when does fear cause human decisions to become less than voluntary; and hundreds more. You may even get some culinary tips—though, I must admit with some disappointment, peanut butter is never mentioned.

More importantly, you'll glimpse in Aquinas the origins of who we are today and what we have come to value. According to Aquinas, humans are, at heart, *thinking* creatures. As Aquinas writes, "The human mind can understand truth only by thinking." As rational, intellectual beings, it is by thinking that we were intended to know right from wrong, to establish the existence of God, to

discover the nature of sexuality, to determine how to set up society, to assess laws, to fight wars, to topple tyrants, and to understand ourselves.

Aquinas taught the world a simple but important lesson, one as valuable today as when Europe was emerging from the Dark Ages: When we employ our reason and intellect as they were designed to be used, the results can only be "godly"; when we reject the human mind and its gifts, the results can only be disaster. How much hate, how much pain, and how much injustice have been created by even sincere, well-meaning believers who have forgotten Aquinas's humble charge to humanity: Use the intellectual gifts that God has given you.

The concept is simple; the implications are revolutionary.

Notes

1. Beginnings: Thomas Aquinas's Life and Times

1. See Jacobus de Vaagine, *Life of St. Bernard* (written about 1250). For a contemporary treatment, see W. T. Jones, *The Medieval Mind* (New York: Harcourt Brace Jovanovich, 1969), 198–201. See pages 190–96 in this volume for more on Peter Abelard as well.

2. Bernard Gui, "Life of St. Thomas Aquinas," in *The Life of Saint Thomas Aquinas,* ed. Kenelm Foster (Baltimore: Helicon Press, 1959), 30.

3. Gui as cited in Anthony Kenny, *Aquinas* (New York: Hill & Wang, 1980), 2.

4. The formal process for canonization—conferring sainthood upon an individual—that is now in place was not instituted until the centuries after Aquinas. The details of the 1319 canonization inquiry of Aquinas can be found in Foster, *Life of Saint Thomas Aquinas,* 82–126. See also Kenny, *Aquinas,* 2.

5. For details about these reports (and lots of other interesting information on Aquinas), check out the Web site of Notre Dame's Jacques Maritain Center at www.nd.edu/Departments/Maritain.

6. Quoted in Kenny, *Aquinas,* 6. For a full-length disputation of the arguments of non-Jews and non-Christians, see Aquinas's *Summa contra Gentiles* (i.e., *Treatise against the Gentiles*).

7. Pope Leo XIII, encyclical *Aeterni Patris,* 1879.

2. Humans, Angels, and God

1. See Thomas Aquinas, *Exposition on Boethius on the Trinity,* exposition III, question 1, article c, and Thomas Aquinas,

Summa Theologica, part I, question 46, article 2. Both references can be found in Vernon Bourke, ed., *The Pocket Aquinas* (New York: Washington Square Press, 1960), 284–88. There are a number of good translations of the works of Aquinas into English. In this volume, I cite Aquinas's section numbers in addition to the page numbers of individual translations so that you will be able to find the passages no matter which translation you are using. The *Summa,* in particular, is such a long work that it is sometimes difficult to locate specific passages within it. It is divided into three main parts, designated by Roman numerals I, II, and III. The second part is so long that it is further subdivided into a first section (designated I-II) and a second section (II-II). I offer some advice with regard to reading Aquinas and the *Summa* in chapter 10.

2. Thomas Aquinas, "Sermon on the Creed," in Bourke, *Pocket Aquinas,* 285–86.

3. Etienne Gilson, "Can the Existence of God Still Be Demonstrated?" in *The McAuley Lectures* (West Hartford, Conn.: Saint Joseph College, 1960), 1–14.

4. Aquinas, *Exposition of Boethius,* II, q.3, a.c, as cited in Bourke, *Pocket Aquinas,* 290.

5. Aquinas, *Summa Theologica,* I, q.2, a.3, as cited in *Introduction to St. Thomas Aquinas,* ed. Anton Pegis (New York: Random House, 1948), 22–27.

6. Gilson, "Can the Existence of God," 9–10.

7. Aquinas, *Summa Theologica,* I, q.2, a.3, as cited in Pegis, *Introduction to St. Thomas Aquinas,* 25.

3. Why Is There Evil? Do Humans Have Free Will?

1. For Aquinas's treatment of the problem of evil, including references to some of these earlier philosophers, see the *Summa Theologica,* I, q.48, as cited in Pegis, *Introduction to St. Thomas Aquinas,* 272–79.

2. *Summa Theologica,* I, q.49, a.2, as cited in Pegis, *Introduction to St. Thomas Aquinas,* 275.

3. Martin Luther, "The Bondage of the Will," in *Martin Luther,*

ed. John Dillenberger (Garden City, N.Y.: Anchor Books, 1961), 203.

4. Aquinas as cited in Anthony Kenny, ed., *Aquinas: A Collection of Critical Essays* (New York: Anchor Books), 261.

5. *Summa Theologica*, I, q.19, a.8.

4. Metaphysics 101

1. *Summa Theologica*, I, q.40, a.1.

2. See Aquinas's discussion in his *Summa contra Gentiles*, III, chap. 2.

5. Law and Morality

1. *Summa Theologica*, I-II, q.90–95.

2. *Summa Theologica*, I-II, q.91, a.1.

3. *Summa Theologica*, I-II, q.94, a.2.

4. Augustine, *Confessions* (New York: Penguin Books, 1961), book 1, chap. 7, p. 28.

5. *Summa Theologica*, I-II, q.94, a.4.

6. The Ins and Outs of Sex

1. For an interesting treatment of Augustine's views on sex, see Elaine Pagels, *Adam, Eve, and the Serpent* (New York: Vintage Books, 1988), 105–14.

2. *Summa Theologica*, I-II, q.153, a. 2, as cited in *Homosexuality and Ethics,* ed. Edward Batchelor (New York: Pilgrim Press, 1980), 39–47.

3. Robert Wood, "Christ and the Homosexual," in Batchelor, *Homosexuality and Ethics,* 165–67.

4. Pope Paul VI, encyclical *Humanae Vitae,* 1968. Pope Paul writes, "The Church teaches that it is then licit to take into account the natural rhythms immanent in the generative functions, for the use of marriage in the infecund periods only, and in this way regulate birth without offending the moral principles. . . . It is true . . . that [in such cases] the married couple are concordant in the positive will of avoiding children for plausible reasons, seeking the certainty that offspring will not arrive . . . but these are just motives."

7. "Just War" and Double Effect

1. George Bush, "The Gulf War," *Wanderer,* 21 February 1991, 6.
2. For a good discussion of the shift in Christian attitudes about violence during this time period, see John Howard Yoder, "The Constantinian Sources of Western Social Ethics," in *The Priestly Kingdom* (Notre Dame, Ind.: University of Notre Dame Press, 1984), 135–47.
3. Augustine, *City of God*, book 19.
4. *Summa Theologica*, II-II, q.40, a.1. For a contemporary discussion, see Paul Christopher, *The Ethics of War and Peace* (Englewood Cliffs, N.J.: Prentice-Hall, 1994), 52–58.
5. *Summa Theologica*, II-II, q.64, a.7, as cited in Christopher, *Ethics of War and Peace*, 57.
6. Ibid.
7. Ibid.

8. Abortion, the Role of Women, and Other Noncontroversial Issues

1. *Summa Theologica*, I-II, q.92, a.1, cited in, *Visions of Women,* ed. Linda Bell (Clifton, N.J.: Humana Press, 1983), 103.
2. Ibid.
3. *Summa Theologica*, I-II, q.165, a.2, as cited in Bell, *Visions of Women*, 111.
4. Thomas Aquinas, *On Princely Government,* Chapter 2, in *Aquinas: Selected Political Writings,* ed. A. P. D'Entreves (Oxford: Basil Blackwell Publisher, 1959), 7.

9. Politics

1. Martin Luther King Jr., "Letter from a Birmingham Jail," in *A Testament of Hope: The Essential Writings of Martin Luther King, Jr.,* ed. James M. Washington (San Francisco: Harper & Row, 1986), 293.
2. Augustine, *City of God*, 18.2.
3. Aquinas, *On Princely Government*, in D'Entreves, *Aquinas: Selected Political Writings*, 2–42.
4. *Summa Theologica*, I-II, q.105, a.1.

5. Ibid. The components of Madison's tripartite system, of course, consisted of the judiciary, legislative, and executive branches (not Aquinas's people, representatives, and monarch), but his goal was similar to that of Aquinas: to moderate the power of any one aspect of government.

6. Ibid., q.90, a.4.

7. Aquinas, *On Princely Government* 6, as cited in D'Entreves, *Aquinas*, 16–17.

8. King, "Letter from a Birmingham Jail," 294–95.

Further Reading

Here are some suggestions for additional reading, starting with works (and edited collections of works) written by Aquinas himself.

Thomas Aquinas. *An Aquinas Reader*. Edited by Mary T. Clark. New York: Fordham University Press, 2000.

Thomas Aquinas. *Introduction to St. Thomas Aquinas*. Edited by Anton Pegis. New York: Random House, 1948.

Thomas Aquinas. *Nature and Grace: Selections from the Summa Theologica of Thomas Aquinas*. Edited by A. M. Fairweather. Louisville, Ky.: Westminster John Knox Press, 1995.

Thomas Aquinas. *Selected Writings*. Edited by Ralph McInerny. New York: Penguin Books, 1999.

Thomas Aquinas. *Summa contra Gentiles*. Translated by Anton C. Pegis. Notre Dame, Ind.: University of Notre Dame Press, 1997.

Thomas Aquinas. *Summa Theologica*. Translated by Fathers of the English Dominican Province. 5 vols. Allen, Tex.: Thomas Moore Publishing, 1981.

G. K. Chesterton. *Saint Thomas Aquinas: The Dumb Ox*. New York: Image Books, 1974.

Frederick Copleston. *Aquinas*. New York: Penguin Books, 1991.

John Finnis. *Aquinas: Moral, Political, and Legal Theory*. Oxford: Oxford University Press, 1998.

Etienne Gilson. *The Christian Philosophy of St. Thomas Aquinas*. Notre Dame, Ind.: University of Notre Dame Press, 1994.

Ralph McInerny. *Ethica Thomistica*. Washington, D.C.: Catholic University of America Press, 1997.

Further Reading

Josef Pieper. *Guide to Thomas Aquinas.* San Francisco: Ignatius Press, 1991.

Jean Porter. *The Recovery of Virtue: The Relevance of Aquinas for Christian Ethics.* Louisville, Ky.: Westminster/John Knox Press, 1990.

Index

Index